HQ650

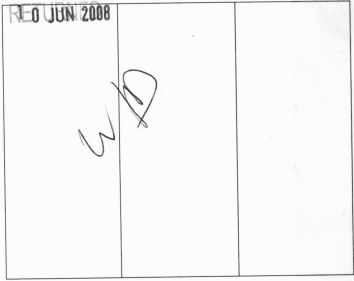

Rev'd
08/12

Mother Courage

Letters from Mothers in Poverty
at the End of the Century

EDITED BY CHRISTINE GOWDRIDGE,
A. SUSAN WILLIAMS
AND MARGARET WYNN

PENGUIN BOOKS
IN ASSOCIATION WITH THE MATERNITY ALLIANCE

PENGUIN BOOKS

Published by the Penguin Group
Penguin Books Ltd, 27 Wrights Lane, London w8 5tz, England
Penguin Books USA Inc., 375 Hudson Street, New York, New York 10014, USA
Penguin Books Australia Ltd, Ringwood, Victoria, Australia
Penguin Books Canada Ltd, 10 Alcorn Avenue, Toronto, Ontario, Canada m4v 3b2
Penguin Books (NZ) Ltd, 182–190 Wairau Road, Auckland 10, New Zealand

Penguin Books Ltd, Registered Offices: Harmondsworth, Middlesex, England

First published in Penguin Books 1997
1 3 5 7 9 10 8 6 4 2

Set in 10.5/13pt Monotype Bembo
Typeset by Rowland Phototypesetting Ltd, Bury St Edmunds, Suffolk
Printed in England by Clays Ltd, St Ives plc

'Poor folk got to have courage . . . Simply getting up in the morning takes some doing in their situation. Mere fact they bring kids into world shows they got courage . . . All I'm after is get myself and children through all this with my cart.'

Mother Courage speaking in *Mother Courage* by Bertolt Brecht (1940)

Contents

Acknowledgements

This is a book of letters and the mothers who wrote them do not need our thanks. It is their book. Only proper names have been changed, to preserve anonymity.

The letters were written in response to an invitation from The Maternity Alliance. We thank all the midwives, health visitors, trades unions and voluntary organizations, the press and media who told mothers about the book. Special thanks go to Sally McMulkin in County Fermanagh. We are grateful to the National Birthday Trust Fund for a grant towards the cost of clerical and administrative work. Since 1928 the Birthday Trust has worked to improve midwifery services and the lives of mothers and babies. Chris Smith and Margaret Adjaye organized the collection of letters and communicated with many mothers, always with efficiency and enthusiasm.

All royalties will go to research or work to persuade governments to give more help to childbearing and to remove anomalies in the benefits system.

Introduction

ANN OAKLEY

'The whole point of this book lies in the letters which it contains;
and it might therefore have seemed advisable to leave the reader
untroubled by an introduction to gather that point from the letters
themselves.' With these words Margaret Llewellyn Davies, General
Secretary of the Women's Co-operative Guild, introduced
Maternity: Letters from Working Women, which was published in
1915. The same could be said of this volume. The two sets of
letters provide a penetrating snapshot of mothers' lives in 1914 and
1995. What counts is the letters themselves; it's *their* testimony
which must be heard.

The letter-writers who contributed to *Maternity* were wives of
members of the Co-operative Guild. Most of their husbands were
in low-paid manual work. The letters were written in response to
a request from Davies for material which could be used in a political
campaign aimed at improving health care and support for poor
mothers and children. Behind the letters in this later volume lies
a similar purpose – they were solicited by the Maternity Alliance
in order to highlight the material and social conditions of mothers
who are hard-up today.

Reading the letters in both volumes, one cannot fail to be
impressed by the enormity of mothers' daily work in bearing and
bringing up children. Even the most sceptical reader must wonder
what kind of society it is that imposes on mothers the obligation
to struggle against such tremendous odds in carrying out what is
universally recognized – at least on the surface – to be a vital social

task. But one of the main challenges to motherhood is precisely this contrast between rhetoric and practice. Mothers and children may be prized on the level of cultural values, but the *actual* social arrangements made for their welfare convey a different message. As a society, we don't support *all* mothers, but only *certain kinds* of mothers. Young mothers, single mothers, and all those unable to manage financially on their own fall into a different category from those who are married, have their children at a respectable age and don't ask for any help from the state. Even the emphasis we give to desirable maternal behaviour such as breast-feeding (known to be linked not only to better health in infancy but in adulthood also) is mediated by other concerns. One of the letters in this volume recounts the tale of a teacher who resumed work after the birth of her second child and went home to breast-feed every lunchtime. The head teacher stood by the door every day waiting to check the time of her return. When one day she was two minutes late he wrote her an official warning letter.

Motherhood is a vexing and difficult subject. As both biological fact and social bond, it stands on the margins between the two domains of nature and culture. Motherhood is thus both wonderful and troubling. There are many factors which affect how motherhood and women are defined. These include: beliefs about the proper behaviour of men and women; the social status of children; attitudes to death and the value of life; medical science and the health-care system; and the role of the state in maternal and child welfare. All these themes impinge on women's experiences of motherhood in different ways.

Between 1914 and 1995, a great deal of literature has been written about women, motherhood, the family, and medical maternity care. But much of this constructs what the American writer Adrienne Rich has called the 'institution' of motherhood – the ways in which mothers are expected to slot themselves into social frameworks and rules defining how they *should* behave. There's only one way to find out just how women *actually* experience motherhood, and that's by listening to what they have to say.

Maternity: Letters from Working Women was a pioneering attempt to bring women's voices to the forefront of the battle to improve the life chances of mothers and babies at a time when few people realized the extent to which poor medical care, inadequate nutrition, poverty and overwork dominated the lives of many women. 'We claim for these letters', said Davies, 'that for the first time are presented in them the real problems of Maternity seen through the women's own account of their lives.' This sequel volume, published several generations later, has a similar mission – to enable women's voices to be heard, at a time when social and economic change and policies towards mothers and children are raising newly urgent questions.

The main question, of course, is why it is still necessary, over eighty years later, to collect together and publicize women's accounts in this way. Surely the situation of mothers is vastly different now?

Continuity and Change

Some key themes reveal themselves in both sets of letters: the effect on women, children and families of poverty; women's unremitting responsibility for housework and children, for making ends meet, for keeping families together; the problem of men, who are both essential and marginal to the whole enterprise of having and bringing up children; the lack of practical support for mothers' work; the trials and tribulations of medical care; and the impact of motherhood on women's physical and emotional health. These themes ring out across the gulf of the generations; here the voices of women are in unison, accusing the social and political fabric of failing to meet their needs. Yet there is also much that's different. The women who penned the 160 letters in the first *Maternity* were a culturally homogeneous group; there were no different ethnicities, no heritage of Afro-Caribbean or Asian cultures, no challenge of racism to complicate the story of motherhood they told. All the letter-writers were married; motherhood was more closely tied to marriage than it is now. There was no health service free at the point of use for anyone then; state support for mothers and the poor had hardly been invented. Unintended pregnancies, more common because of the state of contraceptive technology and poor access to birth-control services, posed a real threat to women's health. Abortion was against the law. Poor housing was a threat to health just as it is now, but in 1914 the concrete housing estates, with little transport to shops and hospitals and riddled with crime and violence, were still to come.

Poor Mothers

The outstanding message, now, as then, is one about motherhood in poverty. Poverty is a fact of life for seven out of ten lone-parent families, and for two out of ten two-parent families; some one in four of all British children live in or on the margins of poverty. One birth in every three is to a family living on means-tested benefits. Between 1971 and 1989 the number of lone-parent families dependent on benefit nearly tripled, and the proportion living on low incomes rose from 50 per cent to 70 per cent. There is ample testimony to the fact and effects of poverty in these letters. One letter-writer lived with her two children in one room with no windows and no electricity, and had to fight 'with the authorities' for adequate housing after her second child spent three months in hospital with respiratory problems. The mother whose husband abandoned her and her children on Christmas Day had just £10 in the house when he went.

Somewhere decent to live is a primary need. In the decade from the end of the 1970s, there was a 240 per cent increase in the number of homeless families in Britain. An eighteen-year-old moved into rented accommodation with her boyfriend, who deprived her of entitlement to benefits by 'committing the ultimate crime and working'. The house they rented was damp, electrically unsafe, and preyed on by burglars (residents on the poorest council estates in Britain face a risk of burglary which is three times the national average). They had to move out and into the sitting room of her boyfriend's parents' house. A 21-year-old who lived in a hostel for the homeless when her son was born writes: 'I was okay with wee Kenneth on my own to start off with, then I started losing my temper at the slightest thing. I never hit wee Kenneth except for the odd taps on the hand for being naughty, like eating the fags . . . Then I found out I was pregnant again . . . Then one day I snapped at wee Kenneth and took a knife to him. I never touched him, I turned on myself and slashed my wrist.' This story has a happy ending, brought about by help from the health visitor and the GP but also, most importantly, by a full-time job for her husband and enough money to provide for the family properly. Trying to be a good mother when circumstances prevent you from being able to provide for your children drives many women to despair.

Current social security benefits provide an inadequate income for mothers and babies. Most women on benefits cannot pay for a healthy diet. Managing materially, physically and emotionally means being very hard on oneself: 'I had to total up my shopping at the supermarket before I reached the check-outs. Even knowing that I only needed a basket and never a trolley . . . made me feel miserable.' Several of the letter-writers include unflattering mentions of the role of the Child Support Agency in failing to help mothers secure from fathers a better standard of living for their children.

Such pinching and saving went on in 1914, but in 1995 there is the additional language of 'loan sharks', 'debts' and 'negative equity'. Maternity poverty now extends to the middle classes, some of whom have been precipitated out of a comfortable lifestyle by unemployment and the cost of home ownership.

Caring for Health?

One of the main reasons for the publication of *Maternity* in 1915 was to advance the argument for a health service that would cover not just employed men but all women and children. The arrival of the National Health Service in 1948 was the answer. Because it provided a universal service, the NHS had a major impact on the health of women and children. Thus, the story of falling maternal and perinatal mortality is partly one of the NHS's success stories. The worst accounts in *Maternity*, of multiple miscarriages and stillborn children, doctors who failed to arrive, devastating haemorrhages, labours lasting several days and ending in instrumental deliveries with permanent damage to women's health, and appalling ill-health suffered in silence after childbirth, are not repeated in the letters in this volume. But there are still problems. 'What was appalling was the hospital care afterwards', says the mother of one son. 'Baby in special care and myself very ill but could I get to see a doctor?!! I waited 24 hours to see a doctor when I was shaking and fainting and then had to be put on a drip because I'd got so ill.' She also encountered the well-known problem of conflicting advice from different health professionals about how to feed the baby.

The availability of sophisticated medical technology can be helpful to women, but it can also be a cause of stress. A mother of three comments that she was given a blood test for Down's syndrome, but was never told the result. She had to ask for it many months later after a lot of anxiety. One of the most poignant stories is from a twenty-year-old who had her first child at seventeen. She was 'treated like a leper' by her doctor and community midwife. Her health visitor, newly qualified with no children herself, *assumed* she couldn't cope. 'The general response was disgust, embarrassment, patronizing attitudes. The birth was 34 hours of hell. I was not told what was happening or asked what I wanted.' These themes of women's rights to be properly informed and consulted, to choose the kind of care they have and whether to have babies at home or in hospital, are entirely new in the history of motherhood.

At the same time, however, the NHS is a crumbling institution which needs to be defended. The centralization of maternity care in large hospitals has meant that they are miles away for many mothers and quite inaccessible for those dependent on public transport. One mother, at the end of her pregnancy, had to walk twelve miles to see her eldest son in hospital. Mothers are the main victims of the public-transport cuts. There are GPs with no time to do antenatal care properly or answer mothers' questions, and community midwives who can't offer proper support for breast-feeding because of cuts in services. Many mothers are very positive about their health care: 'The hospital was great'; the midwife was 'calm, confident and respecting my wishes'; antenatal care from the midwives was 'fantastic. I never met such helpful and supportive people in my life.'

The 1993 report of the Expert Maternity Group, *Changing Childbirth* (the Cumberlege report), reflects many of the points women make about provision for childbirth in these letters. Its central recommendation is that NHS maternity care should become much more 'woman-centred' – sensitive to women's individual needs and respectful of their wishes. Continuity of care, and care which is above all *supportive*, emerges as essential. So does a shift of maternity services back into the community, which is where, after all, they began.

Making Ends Meet

Like the letters in this volume, the literature written by women's organizations concerned with maternity over the last twenty years suggests that there have been real improvements in the way women are treated in labour, but fewer in the area of postnatal care. Many women must get up out of their beds after childbirth and assume the full panoply of their domestic duties with little help from anybody. But lack of support after birth is only the start of the problem; where is the help with child care? A Sikh mother writes that when she went back to work, her parents expected to look after the children, but few women can count on this level of family help. The UK provides publicly funded child care for only two per cent of children under three, compared with 25 per cent in

France and 44 per cent in Denmark. Our level of public child-care provision for under-fives is the second lowest in Europe. A teacher who had her first child at the age of 36 talks of the feeling that she is 'constantly juggling' with her life, trying to be a mother, a home-maker and a wife as well as earning a living in the world of paid work outside the home. Although her partner is helpful, the ultimate responsibility for her child's happiness, security and health belongs to her. 'God knows how they managed without Pampers and convenience foods a generation ago! I worry about the role of women in the future. How can we possibly be expected to cope with everything and do it all?' For those mothers who cannot even afford sanitary towels or other simple necessities this task is daunting.

Housework has changed. Gone are the open fires for heating, the heavy coppers for hot water and washing, the scrubbing board, the communal outside tap and lavatory, the need to buy and cook fresh food every day. The move from 'mangle to microwave' has ushered in an era in which most women can rely on electricity and gas for cooking and heating, on access to automatic washing machines, on running water and inside lavatories, and on pre-prepared commercial foods. This has reduced housework hours, but standards have also risen, increasing the workload of today's home-makers. This is especially difficult for mothers who cannot afford the new conveniences, who have to lug heavy loads of dirty clothes to the launderette and then bring them back wet because they can't afford to use the drier.

The toll on women's physical health of unmechanized homes was obvious in 1914. As Davies put it in her Introduction to *Maternity*, 'People forget that the unpaid work of the working-woman at the stove, at scrubbing and cleaning, at the washtub, in lifting and carrying heavy weights, is just as severe manual labour as many industrial operations in factories.' Today, the same disregard for the labour of housework persists. Most medical studies of the relationship between work and pregnancy outcome only consider employment as work. Many pregnant women who are advised by doctors to give up 'work' in pregnancy actually work harder at home than they did in their paid jobs. The evidence (which is reflected in some of the letters in this volume) is that paid work outside the home is good for mothers' health; it's particularly advantageous for their emotional and mental health, breaking, as it does, the social isolation of the home.

But, most importantly, two incomes are needed these days to provide for children where one would have done earlier in the century. Some of the mothers who wrote the letters in this volume have jobs; others would like to, but are victims of the benefit trap: 'I have given a lot of thought about returning to work, though unfortunately after taking into account outgoings such as bus fares and childminders, there is no incentive to do so.' In most European countries, lone mothers are more likely to be employed than mothers with partners; the UK (along with Ireland and the Netherlands) is an exception. Once in work, women in this country will find that legislation gives them few rights compared with their European sisters. For example, in Italy, mothers in the first year after childbirth have the right to a working day two hours shorter than usual. Income replacement during maternity leave is lower in the UK than in most other European countries.

The expectation that mothers will add paid work outside the home to their several roles inside it marks a discontinuity with the time when *Maternity* was written. Most of the growth in women's employment this century has been in the employment of married women and mothers. At the 1931 census, 10 per cent of married women were employed; by 1987 this had become 60 per cent. A third of mothers of under-twos now have paid work, and nearly half of mothers of three- to four-year-olds. Most of this is part-time work in unskilled or semi-skilled occupations. Motherhood brings demotion in the world of work; half the loss of earnings women incur through motherhood is due to having to take lower-status, lower-paid and often part-time work after having children.

Mothers' Health

In 1914, deaths associated with childbearing in England and Wales numbered 512 per 100,000 live births. Today it is 10. Infant mortality was 105 per 1,000 live births. Today it is 6.2. These 1914 figures were reflected in the questions the 1914 letter-writers were asked to address, which included, 'Did any [children] die under five years old . . . Were any still-born, and if so how many?' One reason that childbirth has become safer is that women have fewer pregnancies. Better availability of a wider range of contraceptive methods has clearly been crucial here. But there is evidence that society is now failing to provide teenagers with the practical sex education they need. Accounts such as that given by one writer, who had two children by the age of fifteen, make distressing reading.

While today's mothers don't write of 'falling' wombs, 'floodings', incontinence, and varicose veins so painful that they can hardly stand, they do write about the physical and mental pain of miscarriages, stillbirths and infant deaths, and about the utter exhaustion and depression that can accompany motherhood in difficult, unsupported circumstances: 'The whole process grinds you down. Every day is a struggle to balance all the demands on you. During this time I have had bouts of depression brought on by the stress of the situation.' Studies of women's health after childbirth show that problems are common. For example, more than one in ten women report extreme tiredness, nearly a quarter suffer stress incontinence, and one in seven backache. Most of these physical conditions last more than a year. So-called postnatal depression affects between 7 per cent and 35 per cent of mothers. In research carried out in urban working-class areas, up to 52 per cent of mothers are depressed. Around 7 per cent suffer the extra difficulties of having a low-birthweight baby. In some poor areas this figure can be as high as 12 per cent.

Social-class inequalities in health were marked in the early years of the century. With the post-Second-World-War Labour government, the start of the NHS and the development of 'the welfare state', the reduction of class inequality became a target of social policy. But since the late 1970s a different policy context has operated, which has meant a widening of the differences between the health and life chances of working-class and middle-class families. Income inequality in the UK is higher now than at any time since the war; the growing proportion of the population dependent on state benefits is a major factor underlying this. One result is that in many areas of the UK the living standards and life opportunities of the poorest are simply unacceptably low. There are many references in these letters to the inadequate diet forced on families by poverty and by the closure of local shops; it is impossible to reach some new large supermarkets without a car. While the impact of this may not be evident in health problems in the short term, the longer-term effects, especially for children, are well-documented.

The Role of Fathers

When it comes to fathers, the message of these letters is a mixed one. There are women who could not cope but for the help and support of their men: 'My Mark's been good with the kids, he does help out with them both'; 'I was a lucky one, I had a man to stand by me.' But some mothers are less fortunate: 'Life with my husband has not been an easy one as he is an alcoholic . . . We have done without a lot because of it'; 'Konrad's father wouldn't give me any money so I had to steal it . . . he used to hit me and make me sleep on the floor.'

The increase in single motherhood is one of the main features of motherhood in the twentieth century. Today in the UK, 25 per cent of live births are to non-married women; this is the second-highest figure of all European countries. Before 1960, the proportion of births to non-married women remained stable at about 4–5 per cent for fifty years, with the exception of the two world wars. Most births to single mothers are to mothers aged under 25. However, single mothers are not necessarily unsupported. The official statistics of family life now feature a new phenomenon – that of 'reconstituted' families. Women who began their mothering careers alone or with their children's fathers may end up living with men who aren't the fathers of their children, and/or with men who have children by other women. Sometimes, as several of these letters witness, these new relationships are a positive force in women's lives, and also create an opportunity for them to move out of poverty.

The UK has the highest marriage rate but also the second-highest divorce rate in Europe. The ethic of the lifetime marriage as the context for child rearing is obviously much less persuasive than it used to be. There are many signs of strain in male–female relationships. Economic factors, especially the increase in unemployment and the growing casualization of labour, impose further stress. While it remains clear what mothers are supposed to do in these circumstances – go on 'coping' and looking after the children – men may react by becoming depressed or defensive: 'My husband feels he can't support us as "a man should" and sometimes I feel irritated that he's not got a "proper" job with a regular wage.' According to studies of the division of labour in the home, unemployed fathers tend to help mothers less, not more.

Historical data on the domestic helpfulness of men are hard to come by. Time-budget studies show that 87 per cent of the care provided for children under five is given by their mothers, and only 13 per cent by their fathers. The increased male pram-pushing noted by social historian Richard Titmuss in the 1950s hasn't been matched by much change in men's willingness to share with women the burden of major household tasks. Having said that, there are few signs in these letters of the privileging of men that went on earlier in the century, with mothers going short of food so that men could have enough.

Love and Courage

Both *Maternity: Letters from Working Women* and *Mother Courage* concentrate on the experience of motherhood for women living in socially disadvantaged circumstances. These women are not the worst off, since at least they had the energy and the resources to write a letter for the book, but their stories are often distressing. What shines through almost all the tales of difficulty, though, is the resilience and courage mothers have in meeting the odds head on and winning as decent a life as they possibly can for their children and themselves: 'As a mother I feel I have done my very best.' Mothers cope; that's the message. 'I may be down a little financially but my spirit is very much alive and well and my lively, kind-hearted, sometimes exasperating children are also an inspiration.' What helps mothers to cope is the strength of the bonds they have with their children. Having children may profoundly disadvantage women in social terms – and it ought not to, given the right social and economic structures and policies. The women who've written these letters are undertaking that most fundamental social task of all – motherhood.

References

V. Beral, 'Reproductive Mortality' (*British Medical Journal*, 1979, 2:632–4)

J. Brannen, G. Meszaros, P. Moss, G. Poland, *Employment and Family Life: A Review of Research in the UK (1980–1994)* (London: Institute of Education, 1994)

G. Brown, T. Harris, *Social Origins of Depression* (London: Tavistock, 1978)

S. Brown, J. Lumley, R. Small, J. Astbury, *Missing Voices: The Experience of Motherhood* (Melbourne: Oxford University Press, 1994)

I. Chalmers, M. Enkin, M. J. N. C. Keirse, *Effective Care in Pregnancy and Childbirth* (Oxford: Oxford University Press, 1989)

N. Chodorow, *The Reproduction of Mothering: Psychoanalysis and the Sociology of Gender* (Berkeley: University of California Press, 1978)

A. Coote, H. Harman, P. Hewitt, *The Family Way* (London: Institute for Public Policy Research, Social Policy Paper no. I, 1990)

N. Cronin, *Families in the European Union* (London: Family Policy Studies Centre, 1994)

Department of Health, *Changing Childbirth* (London: HMSO, 1993)

Department of Health, *Variations in Health: What Can the Department of Health and the NHS Do?* (London: HMSO, 1995)

Department of Health and Social Security, *Low Income Families 1985* (London: DHSS, 1988)

H. Graham, J. Popay, *Women and Poverty: Exploring the Research and Policy Agenda* (London: Thomas Coram Research Unit/University of Warwick, 1989)

C. Hardyment, *From Mangle to Microwave* (Cambridge: Polity Press, 1988)

Joseph Rowntree Foundation, *Inquiry into Income and Wealth* (York: Joseph Rowntree Foundation, 1995)

H. Joshi, 'The Cost of Caring', in C. Glendinning and J. Millar (eds.), *Women and Poverty* (Brighton: Wheatsheaf Books, 1987)

K. Kiernan, M. Wicks, *Family Change and Future Policy* (London: Family Policy Studies Centre, 1990)

J. Lewis, 'Mothers and Maternity Policies in the Twentieth Century', in J. Garcia, R. Kilpatrick and M. Richards (eds.), *The Politics of Maternity Care* (Oxford: Oxford University Press, 1990)

C. MacArthur, M. Lewis, E. G. Know, *Health After Childbirth* (London: HMSO, 1991)

A. Macfarlane, 'Official Statistics and Women's Health and Illness', in H. Roberts (ed.), *Women's Health Counts* (London: Routledge, 1990)

D. McNeish, *Poor Deal: The Cost of Living in the 90s* (London: Barnardos, n.d.)

L. Morris, *The Workings of the Household* (Cambridge: Polity Press, 1990)

NCH Action, *Poor Expectations: Poverty and Undernourishment in Pregnancy* (London: NCH Action, 1995)

A. Oakley, *From Here to Maternity* (Harmondsworth: Penguin Books, 1979)

A. Oakley, 'The Changing Social Context of Pregnancy Care', in G. Chamberlain and L. Zander (eds.), *Pregnancy Care in the 1990s* (Carnforth, Lancs.: The Parthenon Publishing Group, 1992)

A. Oakley, D. Hickey, A. S. Rigby, 'Are Men Good for the Welfare of Women and Children?', in J. Popay, J. Hearn and J. Edwards (eds.), *The Trouble with Men* (London: UCL Press, forthcoming)

A. Phoenix, 'Black Women and the Maternity Services', in J. Garcia, R. Kilpatrick and M. Richards (eds.), *The Politics of Maternity Care* (Oxford: Oxford University Press, 1990)

A. Rich, *Of Woman Born* (London: Virago, 1977)

P. Romito, 'Women's Paid and Unpaid Work and Pregnancy Outcome: A Discussion of Some Open Questions' (*Health Promotion* 4(1), 1989, 31–41)

P. Romito, 'Work and Health in Mothers of Young Children' (*International Journal of Health Services* 24(4), 1994, 607–28)

P. Romito, F. Hovelaque, 'Changing Approaches in Women's Health: New Insights and New Pitfalls in Prenatal Preventive Care' (*International Journal of Health Services* 17(2), 1987, 241–58)

B. K. Rothman, *Recreating Motherhood: Ideology and Technology in Patriarchal Society* (New York: W. W. Norton, 1989)

M.-J. Saurel-Cubizolles, P. Romito, J. Garcia, 'Description of Maternity Rights for Working Women in France, Italy and in the United Kingdom' (*European Journal of Public Health* 3, 1993, 48–53)

R. M. Titmuss, 'The Position of Women', in *Essays on the Welfare State* (London: Allen and Unwin, 1958)

C. Woodcock, M. Glickman, M. Barker, C. Power, *Children, Teenagers and Health* (Buckingham: Open University Press, 1993)

I

'I'm a country mum with little or no money'

I am a very lucky 31-year-old woman, with a partner who loves me, a three-year-old boy and a four-month-old baby girl. My partner works as a tree surgeon and is based just three fields away, and we rent a cottage cheaply from his boss, though it has needed a lot of work on it. For example, we have rewired and put in central heating and landscaped the huge garden. We live by hard work and endurance but at the end of each day, we all have smiles on our faces and know we have done our best.

I'm a country mum with little or no money, so I live for the village bazaars and jumble sales. We have furnished our home from things found in skips and down the tip. Everything from the fridge freezer to the posh carpets has been carted home and cleaned up. I get a great satisfaction on finding a good bargain. We have no transport which is a major problem for me and the kids, as the shops, doctor, etc., are all one and a half miles away, and the food prices are very high. So I grow all my own vegetables, make my own jam, pickles and chutney and dry and sell herbs, etc. My three-year-old son really enjoys helping me and many a happy summer's day was had working in the garden.

My second pregnancy was a living nightmare. I had a low-lying placenta which meant lots of rest, but since I lived miles from any amenities and had a very lively three-year-old, I spent most of my nine months feeling unwell and very depressed and guilty for not being able to get on with things. It was very frightening, being so isolated and with no help, and as I got bigger things got so bad as

I couldn't even walk down the lane, never mind to the doctors. So I missed most of my antenatal check ups, and my partner had to take days off work and borrow cars to get me to the hospital, fourteen miles away, for my many scans. It would have been nice if some back-up system could be introduced for families in my situation like a childminder or transport to the clinic. I asked for help from the local authorities, but unless your child is abused or on the high risk list, you don't qualify.

I finally had a Caesarean birth and stayed in hospital for seven days. We had to pay a childminder for my son during this time, which four months later we are still paying off, as my partner took his two weeks' annual leave when I got home to look after us all. I really worried about my son during my time in hospital which made my stay there awful. The nights were so very noisy with new beds and patients being wheeled in at all hours. It was more like a train station. I couldn't wait to get home just to get a good night's rest.

After two weeks at home my partner went back to work. I was very sore and not very mobile and tired. I needed help even more than before, but none was available. My midwife and health visitors were very kind, but surely in this day and age with so many people out of work, someone could employ helpers for us new mums in a crisis. I feel very angry and let down by the way I was unable to obtain help. Surely one doesn't have to abuse or beat up your kids to get the local authorities calling round with help.

Well, I'm back to normal again now and glad it's all over. My son is pleased to have his daft old mum back again and my baby is enjoying her first real food. But I can honestly say NEVER AGAIN.

'We are coming up to four years of marriage and hope to keep going'

I am married with only two children, Kenneth and Rebecca. I am 21, my husband Kenneth is 22. He works full-time. I have just started working the odd night or two doing Ann Summers. It gets me out and about and away from the children, which you need to do at times.

My husband and I were unemployed when I fell pregnant with Kenneth. He was still unemployed when Rebecca was born which was before we moved up North. My pregnancy was okay with Kenneth. We were living with his mum and dad because we could not afford our own place and there was a waiting list for housing. A month after Kenneth was born, we decided to go into the homeless hostel. We could not stand living with his parents for much longer. It caused a lot of arguments between us. We were housed after two weeks. My husband was unemployed at the time so money was tight. We had £159 a fortnight to live on. That on its own was a hassle and caused a lot of aggro between us.

Things were alright to start off with, then Kenneth was offered a place on a training course which gave us an extra £10 a week. I was okay with wee Kenneth on my own to start off with, then I started losing my temper at the slightest thing. I never hit wee Kenneth except for the odd taps on the hand for being naughty, like eating the fags and playing with the TV and video. I never hurt him. I just shouted and made him cry. I never told Kenneth anything or the doctors or health visitor. I became very depressed easily. Then I found out I was pregnant again. I was on the contraceptive pill, so it was a shock. It got worse during my pregnancy. Then one day I snapped at wee Kenneth and took a knife to him. I never touched him, I turned on myself and slashed my wrist. It was not a deep cut, I covered it up and waited until Kenneth came home. He phoned my health visitor because I refused to go to the doctors. He told my health visitor what happened and she came to see me. I was scared to tell her everything in case wee Kenneth was taken away from me. We talked and she made an appointment for me to go to the doctors as she thought it was postnatal depression. She even looked after wee Kenneth while I went. The doctor confirmed it and gave me mild anti-depression tablets. I got better after long sleeps and talking. I feel embarrassed about what happened. I do not tell people what happened in case they think the worst of me.

My life changed after Rebecca was born, I felt more close to my children. I fed Rebecca myself on demand, which was when wee Kenneth always wanted me. So whenever Rebecca was sleeping I used to give Kenneth all my attention. It worked and he passed the jealous stage and even asked to help change and bathe her. It made me happy. Then we had a bad experience with some neighbours and ended up in the North, where things got better. Kenneth got a full-time job, and we got what we used to get fortnightly, weekly. It was great and now we are happy. The kids are doing great, I am doing great and Kenneth and myself are getting on better than we have ever done. We are coming up to four years of marriage and hope to keep going.

3

'We have had only one holiday
in our lives'

I am a one-parent family. I have four kids – the youngest is one and my eldest is nine. We have had only one holiday in our lives. That was to Ballycastle last year. I had to share the cost with another family and it cost me £100 which I had to save a lot for.

4

'When my daughter goes to bed I turn off the heating'

I have a four-and-a-half-year-old daughter and am struggling to survive on state benefits. I got divorced about eighteen months ago and for the foreseeable future will have to rely on government benefits. I receive £50.93 a week Income Support and £10.20 a week Child Benefit. I find day-to-day living very hard. My main priority is my daughter's wellbeing, which means quite often I go without so that she will have more. She has just started school so it was a struggle to find extra money for uniform and basic school needs. I often have to rob Peter to pay Paul. By that I mean, pay bills, etc., by using money from other bills I have to pay. I have slowly got deeper into debt. It is, I believe, impossible to survive. I do have my own house, which the government pays the mortgage interest on, but what they pay on that comes off my benefit. I am trying to find work, but it is very hard and I've yet to find a job that I can accept. I would like to study so I can get a career but the cost of books and paper, etc. is too costly. I feel in a trap. It's like I'm going round in a circle, getting deeper and deeper into trouble from which I can see no way out. I have constant worries about money. I can never make ends meet. This affects my own wellbeing both physically and mentally.

My daughter doesn't seem affected, as I try to shelter her from all my worries, although this isn't always possible. I would dearly love to come off benefit, but have been unable to as yet. How the government feels I can live on £61 a week I really don't know.

I have to budget carefully, but it isn't always possible. I have to cut back on the basics of life. When my daughter goes to bed, I turn off the heating and make savings like that.

5

'. . . Up at 5.30 a.m. to start again'

I am a single parent with my son since his birth, as he was born in difficult circumstances. I have tried for five years to date to get his father to accept my son as his and to make efforts towards his upbringing but to no avail. My point was that I had put myself and my son through endless years of stress chasing his father, trying to get him to take part in his son's life, that it has just not been worth it and I am saddened as my son now pays the price. He's a beautiful little boy but now he knows that his dad doesn't want him or love him and will say it openly to anyone. He went through months of bad behaviour but appears now to be coming through the other side and changing back to his normal self.

I've always worked since I have had my son and paid thousands of pounds in nursery fees annually for the privilege. People, I feel, fail to realize how hard single parents work, before they get into the office.

I myself used to do the following six days a week. Get up 5.30 a.m., get washed, dressed, get my son washed, dressed, give my son his breakfast. Get the bus at 6.30 a.m., get another bus at 8.00 a.m. to the nursery, then get into work for 9.10 a.m. Leave work at 5.15 p.m., get my son, get the bus at 5.30 p.m., get the bus home at 6.10 p.m., get home at 8.10 p.m., get dinner at 8.30 p.m., get ready for bed at 9.00 p.m. and my son then in bed by 9.30 p.m., then up at 5.30 a.m. to start again. I've had no social life in six years. I used to pay between £200 and £280 per calendar month nursery fees and then have little left to buy food. So you can see that even if you choose to work it's so hard, and particularly hard for me knowing that his father is self-employed, and while I'm struggling, he's off on holidays or out for meals. Eventually I had to leave as I was so far away from work I was spending six, seven hours travelling on buses per day. It was not actually worth it for me or my son.

But there is a way out. What I've decided to do is to accept that his father doesn't want him and will never be a father to him. Instead of channelling my efforts there I've changed the direction of my efforts and put them into starting my own business. It hasn't started yet and I don't know whether it will succeed, but tell other mothers to sit down and think where their efforts are going and if they're not going in the right direction, then change them for the sake of your child. I am still on Income Support and still eating one meal or none a day while I feed my child two meals. But I feel different because I have a goal and am not just plodding on in the dark. If my business idea does not materialize then I am going to try something else.

6

'I fit my work in around when my baby sleeps'

After quite a traumatic pregnancy and losing ten weeks off work on sick leave through a threatened miscarriage, I finished my well-built career as an advertising sales executive for my maternity leave at 32 weeks pregnant. From the moment I finished work, on my leave, I worried about going back to what was a highly dedicated, pressurized job. I had eighteen weeks' paid leave (six weeks at 90 per cent of my salary and twelve weeks at £52.50). Towards the time of my return to work I felt I had no choice in going full-time, as my husband was going self-employed leaving a secure, well-paid job (something which we had planned for some time).

The first shock was the cost of child care. I had chosen a well-reputed nursery where my daughter would have the stimulation of other children. I found I would be paying £85.00 a week with two weeks up front and 52 weeks a year. Even when I would have six weeks' holiday I would be paying for them *not* to look after my baby. My wages would be reduced by about a half. I would have to leave my baby from about 8.15 a.m. until 6 p.m. I sat realistically thinking it through and had outbursts of tears at the thought of having my baby virtually brought up by strangers. As I worked for an international company there weren't any alternatives but going back to the tele-sales department part-time and having a wage drop. Calculating that after child-care fees I would bring home about £25 a week, I embarked on finding a job from home. I found a tele-sales job from home, a new venture for the 100-year-old company I was going to work for. I fit my work in around when my baby sleeps and do paper work at night while my husband looks after her. I had to write a letter to my employer who was expecting me back full-time and had created a more demanding and stimulating job for me. It was like writing a letter proclaiming unfaithfulness.

Money is very tight and I do feel bitter that after twelve years of full-time employment the government doesn't offer a better deal for professional mums to have longer time off (even without pay would do), and employers are losing well-qualified and experienced staff from not looking at more options like job-share or same-status jobs, flexible part-time. I'm sure the experienced staff could produce better results if they were happier with the balance of motherhood/career. When I see mothers who have claimed off the state from the year dot and never had the worry of working because they get paid anyway, it does make me very angry. Flexibility is the key to success.

'No escape from negative equity'

I am the mother of a very bright, well-adjusted five-year-old. Sometimes, I also feel I am the victim of the 1980s housing-market boom–crash, with negative equity of over £15,000 on my shoulders and no easy way to resolve it. I suppose I was one of those people who knew from very early in my pregnancy that I was going to be very much on my own. I was working as a freelance journalist and although I had been with the same company for more than two years, I wasn't entitled to any maternity benefits other than the basic Income Support. I also had no guarantee of work after the baby was born, so I therefore decided to work until just two weeks before the birth.

I had bought my flat, a very modest one-bedroom place in a very ordinary part of London, for £55,000 in 1988, during that extraordinary pressured period of both dismay and optimism when house prices were spiralling at a frightening rate. Like a lot of people, it didn't take much to convince me that if I didn't buy then, I would never be able to afford a home of my own. After just two months of paying what seemed a manageable £409, interest rates began to shoot up and by October 1989 my monthly repayments had increased to £602.

I functioned quite normally at work during my pregnancy, but by the end of the day, once I was on my own, I would be locked in a kind of numbness, spending most of my evenings and weekends in bed, feeling completely isolated. Most of my worry at the time was to do with what I was going to do about money.

I had begun to have problems meeting the payments on my mortgage and I was worried about how I would cope on my own with a baby. It wasn't long before the bottom fell out of the housing market, and by the time my daughter was a year old, my flat was valued at £20,000 below the price I had originally paid for it. I was only unemployed for about six months after my child was born, but I did start getting into serious arrears during that period. I quickly realized that I would never really have enough money to meet all the bills, so I fell into the habit of paying for the things that seemed more pressing with the intention to get the other bills up to date when I had more money. Only there never really is extra money, and once you miss two or three payments it is extremely hard to catch up. I went back to freelancing and after a while I got a long-term placement. But going back to work didn't make things easier, since child-care costs meant that I now had an additional outlay of £375 per month. It was also a highly pressured time, partly because my new job involved some overtime. On those days I would take my daughter to the childminder at 8.30 a.m. and not see her again until 9.30 or 10 at night.

Negative equity in my view is a euphemism for financial and emotional entrapment. Nothing undermines one's life – and indeed one's enjoyment of life – as much as this particular type of financial burden. As well as struggling to pay the bills, keep on working and be a reasonably good mother, there is always the problem of 'the flat'. What do I do with it? How do I get rid of it, meet my financial commitment and remain creditworthy enough to get a badly needed place that will accommodate at least two people comfortably?

I had the flat revalued in 1991, after the slump in the housing market. A sympathetic estate agent suggested (off the record of course) that the best favour I could do myself would be to hand over the keys to the building society. I couldn't. I still needed somewhere to live, and rent and rates in the private sector were at least as much as the mortgage I was paying. Besides, giving the flat up would not relieve me of the £20,000 debt I owed for a property I no longer wanted or wanted to live in. In other words I couldn't move on. I was trapped.

By 1993, my arrears had risen to £4,704; I owed the building society more than I was ever likely to sell the flat for. It got to the stage where I wasn't opening any letters which looked remotely as if they might be demanding payment of a bill. And it wasn't until I was threatened with repossession that I was forced to find an alternative way of dealing with the problem. I realized that the only way that I could continue to meet the mortgage payments as well as pay off the arrears was to rent out the flat and find somewhere cheaper – and even smaller – to live. I have been letting my flat for the past two years, but – even though my daughter has started school and I am paying less for child care – I'm still not much better off. The fact that the rent doesn't pay the mortgage underlines how overpriced it is. My most recent evaluation (September 1995) puts my negative equity at £15,000. Again I am advised that prices are likely to continue dropping so it would be a good time to sell.

If I go with the estate agent's suggestion, I will still be heavily indebted to the building society. I may be able to transfer that debt to another property, but I would be in the same position of paying for a home which is mortgaged way above its market value. It seems there is no escape from negative equity.

'Mend and make do'

My eldest baby is now nearly 22 and is expecting her first baby and my first grandchild in March. There is obviously a world of difference in her pregnancy and maternity care to the one I had while carrying her.

I do not agree with one woman who said her daughter-in-law had to have absolutely everything new for her baby. It's all well and fine if one is financially sound to do so but some of us live on an elastic shoe-string and struggle to make it stretch let alone meet up to tie a bow. There are lots of beautiful baby clothes and items to be purchased second-hand, either from jumble sales or car-boot sales or charity shops. After a good wash most things come up looking good as new. I think parental love and attention and a warm home are more important things to have on your list. When a baby is well cared for, clean and happy, he does not pay attention to what he's wearing or sleeping on.

We managed to exist on my husband's low wage. Yes, I did get family allowance but it was a lot lower than today's. After bills and food we had no social life. After I left work our finances went downhill. It's no joke three living on one wage whereas before you enjoyed life with two living on two incomes. My first pram was a beige one with extras and all for £10. When my second baby arrived I part-exchanged the pram for a dark-green one for £20. I managed to get £5 back from the sale of the beige one. Our navy-blue carry-cot had seen seven babies before the arrival of my first and cost £1.50. I did manage to buy a new navy pushchair, but only because I had it via my friend's club book on weekly payments. I got the new pine cot from my savings just before I left work. Money well spent as it did the two. When they were both in beds, I tied together the two ladder sides of the cot to make a useful clothes horse. When I left work, my mates gave me presents of a bath set and lots of baby-grows. Some relatives and neighbours sent knitted matinée jackets and cardigans. I bought two packs of towelling nappies on offer from a market. I did use disposables but I believe a friend gave me a packet to tide me over the first week I came out of hospital.

My husband was not a lot of help as he was brought up to believe babies are solely woman's work. I bought packs of milk a bit cheaper every second week at the clinic. It was nice to meet other young mums and new babies. Someone gave me a bin bag of odd wool which I managed to crochet into squares to make a pram cover and knitted three scarves to sew together to make a cot cover. I got two rabbit-patterned shawls from my husband's cigarette coupons. I listened to advice from all quarters, said yes, then went home and did my own thing. My first baby was a cry baby and I suffered endless sleepless nights. I was quite prepared for a repeat of the programme with my second baby but was pleasantly surprised to find she was totally opposite and very happy and placid. I bought a lot more baby clothes and covers and a changing mat at school jumble sales. My best bargain buy was a wooden safety gate for 20p. When it was no longer in use, I cut it in half and glued on four small legs and added a top oblong of wood and made my two girls two doll's beds. I got a lot of my ideas and strength from my mum as she came from an era that had to mend and make do. Her mum reared seven children single-handed after being left a widow with the youngest child being only six months old.

My eldest daughter's baby is due in about three weeks. Her hubby is on a low wage. They know they can get family allowance when the baby is born but in the meantime they struggle to get the baby clothes and equipment, and like me she loves bargain-hunting at jumbles and car-boot sales. She would dearly love to be able to buy everything new. At the end of the day love is priority, followed of course by food and bills.

I am looking forward to being a grandma but I know my place and no way will I interfere. All I'm looking forward to is lots of cuddles. I'm currently knitting for the expected bump and if I don't get a move on he will be at school before I've finished it.

9

'. . . Then he was made redundant'

I'm a married mother with two children, John eleven and a half and Alison two and a half. At one time my husband and I had no real money worries but then he was made redundant. He is a quantity surveyor and we never thought for one minute anything like this would land on our doorstep. We had to use all of our savings, and with the help of the family we survived. My husband is now back in employment. He has lost £6,000 in going back to work. Everyone seemed to think that because he was out of work he would be willing to take any wages that were thrown in his face. We struggle from wage to wage, the cost of living now has increased yet my husband's salary, which has to support the four of us, has stayed at the minimum. We do own our own home, we do need to move, but are caught out due to his boss refusing to pay a decent wage. My husband works from seven in the morning until very late at night, with no extra money, no petrol allowance, and his boss knows he is a dedicated worker and underpaid.

We find it hard feeding us all and we have no social life at all. No meals out, no family treats, no hairdos, nothing, it is a depressing time for us all. Food is so expensive and clothes for the children are out of this world. John starts school in August, I haven't a clue how to clothe him. I know we're not the worst off but that doesn't help us to try and cope each month. I did try and get a job but my health deteriorated and I have a lump in my throat (goitre) and at the moment I take each day as it comes and we manage just. I know many families feed hand to mouth and if the cost of living continues to increase while wages stay the same, people will turn to crime and health will go downhill. My husband and I sometimes have gone without food, just to feed our children. Our motto is: It won't stay like this for ever — surely there are better times ahead again.

'I feel like a prisoner'

I find it hard being a mum of three and one on the way. My husband was made redundant three and a half years ago, just after my first son was born. Money was not too bad then because we had saved and got his bits. Now money is very tight and I do not get any help from either side of the family or from anybody professional. My husband is no help, he believes a woman's place is in the home doing everything. He has never changed a nappy or got up to any of the children since they have been born. He goes out fishing every chance. Neither of us smoke or drink. So he feels we can afford it. I don't believe in abortion but I wish that I had had them, as now at 22 years of age with nearly four children, I feel a prisoner.

'A black eye, two young children, a single suitcase and a police escort'

When I left my husband after eleven years of marriage it was with a black eye, two young children, a single suitcase and a police escort. It had taken me a long time to reach the end of my tether but when I did it was in the clear knowledge that there would be no going back – from that point onwards I was taking sole responsibility for our future. I was determined to escape the physical and mental abuse that had been part and parcel of my life for so long and which was starting to have its effect on my young family.

In retrospect, financial considerations seem of little consequence, so dire were our circumstances, but at the time it was very important to me that I should be able to support us. I didn't want to become totally dependent on the benefit system. I had been employed part-time in a hospital doing a job that I felt was worthwhile and which I very much enjoyed. However it wasn't very well paid. Leaving home meant an end to the child-care arrangements that I had organized for when I was at work. My children were aged three years and nine months and as a single parent the question of whether or not I could afford to continue to work was now very much an issue. I knew I could not expect maintenance unless I agreed to my husband's access arrangements and although at first I tried to go along with these, it became increasingly impossible. The net result was that I needed to be able to provide for myself and two children on my 20-hours-a-week salary.

After several months of getting some sort of order back into my life, I returned to my job. An affordable rented flat was a big asset as was getting hold of a cheap but reliable car that saw me through the next few years without major repair bills. My very supportive family helped to make our new flat a home. I shall always be grateful to them and to the friends who fulfilled the old saying about a friend in need . . . ! A gift of some old towels or a dilapidated chest of drawers may not seem like much but to me these things were a godsend.

Another big asset proved to be my eligibility for Family Credit. This enabled me to make ends meet on my part-time salary. Without it I would have been faced with the stark choice between finding full-time employment (and leaving practically all the child-care to paid helpers) or give up work and live on Income Support. After the traumas we had all been through I needed to maintain my self-esteem and my job helped enormously. Also my children didn't deserve to be deprived of a second parent by my working through most of their waking hours. Giving up work would have meant more time with Martin and Emma but with no spare money for outings and treats, and with worries about heating bills if you stay at home, the option didn't seem very desirable. As it was we could have the best of both worlds – I had my afternoons and evenings free to spend with the children, I wasn't as totally shattered as I would have been with a full-time job and I was able to continue working and enjoy the advantages that my work gave me.

I don't think I actually gained financially by being on Family Credit because of all the child-care costs. These can now be taken into consideration when income is assessed but this was not so at the time. At one point I was paying £60 a week out of my salary. Running a car was vital as it enabled me to make the convoluted journeys between home, nursery school, childminder and work that had to be incorporated into my daily schedule. There has been very little spare cash for clothes, but again thank heavens for friends and relatives and for car-boot sales and charity shops. I have become a great believer in recycling clothes and we all manage to look well dressed without hardly ever buying anything new. Thankfully I have managed to stay out of debt and the need for a car means that it is there to use at weekends and for holidays – having a far-flung family and friends who live in lovely parts of the country is great when we need to get away from our flat and inner-city life. We have also been able to take advantage of the extra benefits attached to being on Family Credit. I have attended adult-education classes free of charge and we all make the most of a local-authority scheme which gives reduced-price admission to local sports facilities and even the odd free ticket to a nearby theatre and arts centre.

After four years I am now about to come out of the benefit system. With both children going to school full-time, I have increased my hours at work and hence my salary. I still finish work in time to collect the children from school and so we continue to make the most of after-school visits to the park and the swimming pool. My career has not had to stagnate and with the extra skills I have acquired via the adult education system, I look forward to better prospects when I feel we are all ready for me to work full-time and move on.

I now feel as though I am worlds away from the day when I had to carefully choose what to pack into the single suitcase with which we started our new life. I have no regrets as I know that I am happy, my children are safe, secure and happy and we can all look forward to whatever the future may have in store.

12

'I am selling what things I can'

My boyfriend and I had just moved into a new flat together. We were both nineteen years old and, I suppose, very naïve. We often talked about children and marriage, and what we would do if I fell pregnant. We decided we would stay together, because we loved each other and it's both our responsibility. But when the crunch came and he told his mother, he tried to force me into an abortion. He said he still loved me and always will. But within a week of our break-up (I refused an abortion) he was sleeping with an ex-girlfriend of his. My family were not speaking to me because of other reasons, my best friend was away at college, so I had no one. I began to hate the baby and I wanted rid of it because it ruined my life. I would thump myself in the stomach and lean on things with my stomach. I tried starving myself and each time I tried I was hearing a little voice inside my head saying 'Please don't hurt me, mummy', and I would cry. I had even made an appointment for an abortion but I couldn't go through with it. As soon as I decided I would keep and love my baby I felt better and happier, I even began to feel excited and thoughts about not having a baby didn't exist.

I suffered badly with colic and morning sickness. I was in and out of hospital and unable to work. But it will all be worth it. I now suffer with unusual cravings and being cold all the time and financial worries. I get £35 a week of Income Support and my rent paid. Most of my money goes on the electric and gas meters (£15 a week at most, depending on the weather), a minimum of

£15 a week on food (as there are only particular things I can keep down) and the rest on bus fares to the hospital. I cannot afford to buy maternity wear (second-hand) or baby equipment. I'm selling what things I can afford to part with, TV, books and jewellery. I'm now selling my typewriter which breaks my heart because I want to be a writer. Sacrifices have to be made, I keep telling myself.

Though I suffer and struggle, and I nag my present boyfriend, who is being wonderful keeping me sane, my life feels like hell and I'm constantly depressed. Nothing can take away the funny excited feeling I feel when I dream of holding my baby, and when I feel it kick. I'm definite it is a girl but everyone else thinks it's a boy. I don't really mind as long as it's healthy and it loves me as much as I love it. It's all worth it, it gets you ready to enter the real world. I would not advise getting pregnant, not until you're at least ready, both of you and you are happy. That's important to you all.

13

'The first year of our baby's life has been wonderful'

I am 34. I was struggling with an acting career before I got pregnant but was thinking of giving it up, and started a degree (part-time) to help find a new, less insecure, career. My partner and I had not been together long but we were both sure we wanted children from the beginning. I am writing anonymously because I will tell you that we could not afford to admit that we were more or less living together. He has a mortgage with negative equity and was also changing professions. I have my own mortgage and the only feasible thing was to look like a single parent for the first year, until he (or both of us) could find enough to support us, as a couple/family. I feel women's non-status once they are treated as man and wife is one of the major sexual injustices – we do not even count as unemployed if we have a partner!!

This said, the first year of our baby's life has been wonderful. He's good tempered and fun and I feel I've done OK so far as a mother. Luckily I've had lots of clothes and toys passed down from cousins, and so I haven't felt too worried about money, although it's future years – education, nurseries, etc. that worry me. I can't imagine how any women can afford to go back to work, and it horrifies me that we are not guaranteed any nursery education – the idea that the only educational stimulus until five – such formative years! – might be the mother (who might not be able to stimulate the young imagination if she herself is badly educated!!). Also the idea of having an active under-five 24 hours a day without a break!! Much as I love my son, and want to encourage him as well as entertain, I know that without some breaks the time I have with him will not always be quality time, especially as he demands more. I think I would end up screaming and/or ignoring his demands just to give myself some space. I would also be far more likely to lose any sense of myself and any self-confidence. I am determined to get him a part-time nursery or playgroup place, hopefully by the time he is two. I also wouldn't want him to be educated full-time by someone else, so the balance is important to me. I cannot imagine only seeing him evenings and weekends, I love to watch each new development and encourage him – but I do need space for myself as well.

I am fairly impressed with the amount of places to take a toddler. Many of the one o'clock clubs are good – as are some mother-and-toddler groups. It has helped to meet other mothers in the area as I did feel extremely isolated to start with. I would love to live in a town with more community spirit, it is only now as a mother that I've started to know any neighbours, and it takes quite a while to establish friendships. My main fear during this first year is that I feel my self-confidence slipping away. I am losing touch with all my professional single friends and look at myself as 'only a mother'. When low I feel I have nothing but baby talk to say and am clutching on to the part-time degree as a lifeline. Other times I feel optimistic and happy with my choices and that I will get more of my own life back when he is older.

I worked through some of my pregnancy and felt well and looked after – went to a few yoga classes, saw the doctor occasionally, ate lots! Then my baby was born prematurely – a great shock. The birth itself was (in retrospect) not too bad considering. I was very sorry that I wasn't allowed to give birth squatting because they were worried about the baby – and that I couldn't have a bath or walk around the room during labour, because of the monitor on the baby's heart all the way through labour, but I did it with only TENS [Transcutaneous Electric Nerve Stimulation] and gas and air. One of the midwives was very caring, the other officious and intimidating, but I felt safe. My partner was wonderful, supportive throughout.

What was appalling was the hospital care afterwards. Baby in special care and myself very ill but could I get to see a doctor?!! I waited 24 hours to see a doctor when I was shaking and fainting and then had to be put on a drip because I'd got so ill. The different departments seemed unable to liaise. When baby was moved to transitional care they didn't tell me. I wanted to breast-feed and had to request information continually. I was eventually told 'the breast-pump's in there' – half the pieces were missing and no one came to show me how to use it. There was I lying on my own, with a tiny baby in special care, a long walk away, which I felt too weak to face unless I had visitors (in case I fainted). The emotional impact of being surrounded by all the other mothers with their babies was horrific. Yet no one had time to check how I was or talk to me about him.

In transitional care I saw other mothers getting worse treatment – or babies being ignored. I was given different advice on feeding (he was taking some breast milk and some through a tube in his nose). Each midwife or doctor said something different – 'He's not very strong, you'll starve him if you only breast-feed and he'll have to go back to special care' – 'He's got to learn to suck. If you keep feeding down the tube, you'll never get to take him home – he can't go home till he's feeding himself', etc. I was so stressed I cried each time my poor boyfriend appeared and he was stressed because he had to go home leaving us both there each night. Eventually, I was told we could take him, and then we waited for six hours before we could be discharged, having been given a time earlier that day.

Once we were home I felt what it was like to be looked after. I relaxed while friends and family visited and my partner and I could at last lie in bed with our little baby between us. I've never been so glad to get away from somewhere as from that hospital. A home birth next time for sure! He slept a lot for the first month (because of being premature) so I got a lot of rest and didn't feel guilty about taking naps during the day. I wonder how I'll manage with a second child (which I would now like) because I needed so much rest myself. I feel that I am quite spoilt, with a caring partner who is very involved with the child, and a sister nearby who I sometimes do babysitting swaps with. It would be wonderful to have grandparents close (as we don't get out of an evening all that much) but one can't have everything and I go to college some evenings anyway.

My partner and I have to consciously give ourselves some time, and I can see how easy it would be to become argumentative, because so much attention goes on the child and not on each other. But we are conscious of this and are still very caring to each other. And rejoice daily in the health and happiness of our little one. We are finding the places – pubs that accept young kids, swimming pools, parks, etc. – that we can go to as a family and are adapting to a totally new way of life.

Health wise, he's had all his injections, and not had bad reactions. I'm glad he no longer has to go for regular baby clinics as we used to queue for so long at the doctors, but the local surgery is family friendly and the one time I rang frightened at night, the doctor came out and put my mind at rest. I enjoyed a baby-massage class run by a local surgery and an exercise class (with the babies lying on mats in front of us) run by our local hospital and it was good to have weekly events to structure the days with as it's been strange to be out of work and not looking for work.

It seems mothers today divide so between those who go back to work and suffer all the guilt and worry of childminders or nurseries, and those who stay at home and suffer lack of self-confidence and a feeling of inferiority. 'Oh, I'm just a mother!!' The divide is quite hard on friendships too. I don't know quite what solution there is to this. For myself part-time work would seem to be an ideal solution, but part-time childminding is hard to find and expensive. I'm also very aware that the few men I know who have chosen to be the childrearers (while their partner works) are very disadvantaged. Not only are mother-and-toddler groups not called parents and kids, but crèches are often on women-only mornings at local leisure centres, etc. As more men do share in child rearing, perhaps it will be recognized as the important and difficult occupation it is.

'We have no savings as we have been bringing up children for 27 years'

I had my first baby in 1968, my second in 1976 and third in 1978. After my third baby was born we decided we could not afford any more, so my husband had a vasectomy. Then in 1986 at the age of 40 I became pregnant again. My husband's vasectomy had rejoined itself after eight years. It was such a shock even my GP said there was no way I could be pregnant and to go home and forget about it, so I did. Then when I started to put on a lot of weight I bought myself a home-testing pregnancy kit and it was positive. I was seventeen weeks pregnant. We have had to struggle ever since. I can honestly say that it costs as much now to bring up one child as it did to bring up three in the sixties and seventies. I will be 50 this year and my husband 54. We have no savings as we have been bringing up children for 27 years so far and Hayley has got a long way to go before she leaves school. I think we should have got compensation. After all, when you have a vasectomy you don't think you will end up with another baby.

'I am not a scrounger'

I am 29 years old and married to Keith who is 39. Keith has two children aged eleven and eight from his first marriage. They live near us with their mother and we see them frequently. Our children are Rebecca who had her third birthday last week and Susan who is fifteen months old. We live in a two-bedroom terraced house that we have a mortgage of £31,000 for, which is about half the value of the house. I have chosen not to work and to stay at home with the children. Keith has been an actor for 22 years, but has had very little work for the past two years, so we have been living on Income Support during this time.

When I was pregnant with our first child I was working as a trade journalist earning £15,000 a year. Since Keith was always in and out of work we led a modest lifestyle as we could never depend on his income. We had bought our house two years before as a semi-derelict heap, so most of our money went on renovating it. Keith also had £30 a week maintenance to pay his other children. I took my full 39 weeks' maternity leave and returned to work part-time while Keith looked after the baby. We couldn't afford a childminder and I couldn't trust a stranger to look after Rebecca anyway. It was a disaster. Keith resented being a 'nanny' as he put it. I felt as if I was being torn to pieces every morning when I walked out the door and left a grumpy husband and crying baby. Rebecca changed from being a happy baby into being unsettled. After two weeks I handed my notice in. Luckily I was offered a career break, when I could officially resign but could have my job or its equivalent back after five years, on condition I work two weeks a year to keep up to date. It seemed the ideal set up, although I don't seem to have any legal standing with it. I was very keen to have another baby soon as I'd been close in age to my sister and we'd been great friends. On Rebecca's first birthday I started awful morning sickness. At this stage our standard of living wasn't too bad, we'd just about finished the house and Keith had had some TV work that paid well. This was the beginning of 1993. Since then he's only had odd days of work, and anything he earns is immediately deducted from our benefit so we end up no better off. His ex-wife is always pressing for money, which when she gets she squanders on stupid things, which I resent.

We eat okay but very simply, meat is an occasional treat, we eat lots of pulses and pasta, tons of fruit and vegetables. I'm obsessive about getting enough fresh fruit and vegetables inside us. We rarely go out and I've lost some friends through this as money they would spend without noticing on an evening could feed us for a week. We don't buy records, or have a regular newspaper, I usually cut my own and the children's hair and I hardly ever get new clothes, but have discovered the joy of buying a jumble-sale bargain. Keith's parents are very generous, they are too old and ill to be of much practical support but they have us round for Sunday lunch and give us £30 or so occasionally if we're really stuck. They help out with Keith's older children, buying them shoes among other things. They took us to a holiday cottage in Suffolk last year and this year instead of a birthday present for me, my family and Keith's family are paying for a holiday cottage for a week, so we do get holidays. My parents live by the sea so the girls get a beach holiday when we go to see them. Before I had the girls I travelled abroad with my work a lot. At the moment I'm not worried that we can't take them abroad as the hassle would outweigh anything we'd gain from it. Equally while the girls are young and not sleeping well I'm too tired to want to go out much in the evenings.

When I was eighteen weeks pregnant with Susan, I started bleeding and ended up in hospital for a morning. I remember most how wonderful it was to be able to lie down and do nothing for a while. I was very tired. Rebecca wasn't walking yet so I had to carry her a lot and the all-day morning sickness had got me down. I had a scan which showed the baby was fine. This is something I now regret as I subsequently had two other scans as the hospital didn't agree with me on my dates. Since then there have been studies published that suggest multiple scans can affect the baby. I wish I'd had more strength to believe that she was alright and not needed the mental prop of seeing her on a TV screen. During both pregnancies I was extremely careful about what I ate, especially in the early days, and what I exposed myself to — cigarettes, petrol-pump fumes and exhaust fumes.

I had wanted to have my first baby at home, but my GP told me this was impossible. Because I wasn't clued-up as I am now I gave in, but did stand my ground enough to have a domino delivery [in and out of hospital very quickly]. In theory I should have known my midwife by the time of the birth, but she was off duty so I ended up with a stranger. She was jumpy and frightened of the absent consultant as if he were some god. I didn't want any intervention but because the labour lasted so long she talked me into having my waters broken. There was meconium in the amniotic fluid so hospital policy stated I had to have a foetal scalp electrode. I hate the idea of metal clips digging into Rebecca's scalp. I was also tied to the machine from then on, which gave an unreliable readout. Keith stayed with me throughout and tried his hardest to be supportive, but I would probably have been better at standing up for myself without him there. He had had a baby born dead with his first wife so was terrified the whole time and wanted every bit of medical intervention just in case. It ended up with me in full contractions reassuring him everything would be OK. At least I held out against pain relief. In a 23-hour labour I had nothing, not even gas and air, so that Rebecca had no drugs in her when she eventually slithered out. I couldn't get up to squat, I was tired but I knelt up to push her out. I instantly ripped my T-shirt off and held her against me all bloody. It's all a blur as they had to check her lungs were clear of meconium but she was fine and breast-feeding within minutes. She finally stopped breast-feeding at thirteen months. I needed a couple of stitches so they strapped my legs into undignified stirrups. The midwife was concerned that I cover up my breasts as it was a young male doctor who was going to stitch me up; yet he was about to peer at my genitals! I thought I had better be very nice to him as depending on how well he stitched me could make a difference to my sex life in future. Three hours later, at four o'clock in the morning, we gingerly drove home and at half-eight the phone calls and visitors started. Later in the morning I remember my 43-year-old sister-in-law sitting in the bedroom with her family, not knowing quite how to react to me breast-feeding in front of them – she's the sort who can't even mention the word 'period' without deep embarrassment.

I'd been totally unprepared as to how much I'd bleed afterwards and ran out of maternity pads within hours, so my 70-year-old father-in-law was despatched to find a chemist open on a Sunday morning. He was very embarrassed and ended up writing 'sanitary towels' down on a piece of paper and pushing it over the counter to the chemist. The following day my mother came to stay for a week. She bought us a cot and cleaned, cooked and washed for us. The midwife came round for the first ten days, I was terrified of her seeing the house in such a state – we were sleeping on a blow-up mattress and still renovating the place. She was always in too much of a hurry to notice anything or for me to feel I could ask for help if I'd needed it.

Rebecca was, and still is, a robustly healthy child. I took her to the clinic a few times, but after they'd managed to misplot her height on a graph, which put her as dangerously underweight, and not noticed it, and then given me contradictory advice about feeding her – including saying I was breast-feeding her too much – I packed in going. The scales they used were cold and frightened Rebecca, the length measurer was cold and hard and they insisted on making the babies wait around with no clothes on. I never took my second daughter to the clinic.

My relationship with Keith took a nose-dive after Rebecca was born. It was three months before I dared to attempt intercourse and then it was painful for months after. We were always completely knackered so on short fuses and by the time we got to bed, all I wanted to do was sleep. I was totally wrapped up in Rebecca and had strong ideas about her care – no formula milk, no baby food with sugars or additives, no leaving her crying in the cot, no TV, so I didn't give him room to develop his relationship with her. Equally I think he was frightened of Rebecca after the bad time he'd had in his first marriage, when he hadn't been allowed near the children. I insisted he should play his part, but it took a long time for him to have any confidence with her. Breast-feeding was an issue between us as he'd say the only way to shut her up when she started crying was to shove a breast in her mouth, something he couldn't do. Apart from this I found breast-feeding easy and enjoyable, after the initial sore nipples and constantly soggy T-shirts. Rebecca thrived. I enjoyed watching the shocked expressions as I got on with it in trains, cafés, parks, shops, but nobody ever asked me to stop and only once to go elsewhere (in a café). One of the joys of breast-feeding was that my periods didn't arrive until about nine months after the birth. I am glad that I've provided both girls with the short- and long-term health benefits of being breast-fed. Little by little since Rebecca was born Keith has taken a more equal share of the housework and caring for the girls. But he will never do the nappies.

Susan's birth was wonderful. This time I held out for a home birth. I had a 40-minute argument with my GP about it, but at least he didn't strike me off and we agreed to differ since. I chose to have my antenatal check ups at home or at the surgery, which-ever suited. At eight o'clock one Saturday morning I woke up in labour, phoned my parents who got on the first train from Lanca-shire to London and phoned a friend who drove down from Wolverhampton; then just got on with my day, eating lots, playing with Rebecca and having friends round for coffee. My parents and my friend made it in plenty of time. Again my assigned midwife

was off and again it was the same midwife I'd had for Rebecca.
In my own home she couldn't have been different, calm, confident
and respecting my wishes. Another lovely midwife chose to come
along even though it was her night off. This time labour lasted
nineteen hours. Rebecca fell asleep on my father's knee downstairs
and the midwives, Keith, my mother and my friend took over
upstairs.

Again there was meconium in the amniotic fluid when my
waters finally gushed out of their own accord in the early hours
of Sunday morning, but the baby was fine. Afterwards we all sat
round the bedroom eating chocolate cake and drinking coffee,
there was no hurry to get myself sorted out as I didn't need to go
anywhere, I was home already. Every sheet and towel in the house
was covered in blood and the placenta sat in a black plastic bin
bag in the outside loo until the following Thursday, which was
bin day. I had squatted while pushing Susan out so I needed no
stitches. It was also very important to me that I hadn't had to leave
Rebecca at all. Being in my own home surrounded by people who
I loved and trusted made the birth fulfilling. I sucked strength from
everybody and this time Keith was brilliant. Susan weighed 9 lb.
exactly. Fifteen months later I still haven't had an unbroken night's
sleep. Her first year is a haze of tiredness and the slog of looking
after two small people who are totally dependent on me. I am still
breast-feeding her, consequently illnesses seem to bounce off her.

I don't at all regret my decision to stop work. Watching other
women who chose to go back to work or felt financial pressure
to, their children are not as happy as mine, their children are ill
more often and are not as bright and outgoing. The women are
constantly pulled in two directions. These children are paying a
high price for their mothers' careers or financial status. I am lucky
that we are able to afford to survive on Social Security for a while.
My children are happy, healthy and well-balanced. I am not a
scrounger, the government should be prepared to support women
who choose to stay with their children in the early years when
the patterns of a child's personality are being formed. There is too

much pressure on women to do it all and go back to work far too soon after having a baby, emotionally damaging their children and probably themselves. The important task of nurturing is left to someone else. Being a nurturer is not less important, less demanding or less of an achievement than having a successful career.

For the next few years I am restricted to living in a tiny house. We do have a small sunny garden, but we get noise and vibration from huge lorries thundering past on the main road behind us. Often in summer, I have to bring the girls indoors and shut all the windows because a factory is polluting the air so much it makes us choke. I worry what the pollution is doing to the girls' lungs. We are fighting to stop the lorries and the pollution, but if this were not a working-class area would these problems have been allowed to develop? One day I'd like to live in a house with a bedroom each for the girls, away from the pollution and busy roads, where the schools have enough teachers and the parks are not full of broken glass. I am lucky I chose to live on Income Support and I have the skills to get off it once the girls start school. I wish the government would help those who haven't the choice.

16

'I have to work 104 hours a week to get a wage of £208'

I am a mother of five children whom I love very dearly. I am aged 34 years. I was married at sixteen, my husband was 28 years old. I had my first child in the first year of my marriage. I was only sixteen years of age. During my first pregnancy, my husband worked. After I had my son, when he was six months old I took a part-time job. I worked right up until I was five months pregnant with my second son so I was entitled to Maternity Allowance of £18.50 per week. When my second son was three months old my husband lost his job, so we had to go on Social Security benefit. When I fell pregnant with my third son I was working part-time, I worked right up until I was eight months pregnant and then had to give up my job so we had to go back on Social Security. I applied to the Social Security for a grant to get a pram and cot and layette for my baby but was refused.

All I was given for my third baby was £25 Maternity Grant and told to buy a pram and cot and layette out of it. My third son used to sleep in a drawer because we had no money to buy the things that we needed for him. We were living off £21 Social Security and £13 Child Benefit. We did not have any money but we were happy and had three beautiful healthy sons. Things were improved by the time I had my fourth baby which was a beautiful daughter. We were off Social Security. My husband was working full-time until 1990, when he had an accident at work which left him with a bad back. I was on a training course at the time trying to get a SCOTVEC [Scottish Vocational Education Council] and looking after four children when I found out I was pregnant with my fifth child, which was a surprise as I was told that I could not have any more after my fourth. By the time I had my fifth baby we were back on Social Security. We were given £100 Maternity Grant to buy a pram, cot and layette for my baby.

My first pregnancy was a normal pregnancy but the birth was a forceps delivery. My second pregnancy I was sick for the full nine months but it was a normal delivery. My third pregnancy was normal but it was a section delivery. My fourth pregnancy was normal and so was the delivery. My fifth pregnancy was difficult, I was in and out of hospital for the nine months that I was pregnant but the delivery was normal.

We did not have any spare money, it was a struggle to bring up five children on Social Security but we plodded on and when my fifth baby was six months old I went out to look for a job in Security as I have a SCOTVEC in Security. I have been working since my son was six months old and am still working. I am very low paid but I'd rather be working than on Social Security. We have never got any spare money but we try to give our children the things that they ask for. We have a lot of love to give to our children. If I had it to do all over again I would not change a thing about my life or children or the struggle that we have to bring up five children. They are my life and I love them and my husband very much.

My husband and sons go to clubs and away on holidays to camps. The clubs and camps are run by a charity called FARE. If I had to pay the full amount for the boys and my husband to go on holiday they would not be able to go. My husband goes as a cook so he does not have to pay anything. The boys only have to pay £15 each – the total cost of the holiday is £65 each but FARE pays the other £50 for them. My daughter was away on holiday from 9 July to 16 July to Teen Ranch. The cost of the holiday was £95 but I only had to pay £15 for her, FARE paid the other £80.

I have had money problems since January 1995. I got into trouble with loan sharks. I borrowed money from them at Christmas to get things for my children's Christmas. I pay them £100 a week. If I miss it one week more interest goes on it. I have to work 104 hours a week to get a wage of £208, tax and insurance comes off, that leaves me with about £160. I have to pay back £100 to loan sharks that leaves me £60 and £35 Child Benefit to live on. I never have any spare money for luxuries. I only get £2 an hour for the job I do in Security. I find it very hard to make ends meet. I have to buy food, powercards, gas, clothes off £95. I cannot afford to go on holiday myself but I make sure that my children go on holiday and that is the only luxury. I would dearly love to go on holiday but that is out until next year as by that time I will be clear with the loan sharks. My children and husband come first as I have to work all the time to make ends meet.

'Extra challenging as I am disabled'

When I began this pregnancy I didn't see myself as on a terribly low income, and thought we were managing on my half pay from maternity leave. I thought I would go back at least temporarily to the job and look for something else. But life intervened; the funding for my post was not renewed, meaning I was made redundant, closely followed by my husband becoming seriously ill. So suddenly I was a single parent, extra challenging as I am disabled and a wheelchair user myself. I'd always said I had absolutely no wish to be a single parent, and that's still true. I am permanently drained and do nothing except look after Ben in the best way I can, given the restrictions on us. It's better now but a few months ago we were on minimal benefits and I worried all the time. People say they need shoes every six weeks at this age. I didn't know how we'd manage it and a holiday – well, it has to be accessible to me as a wheelchair user as well as baby-friendly, preferably with a babysitting service. So that means not the cheapest packages. It's out of the question at present. When planning this I thought we'd have an au pair, but we haven't been able to move to somewhere big enough to make that possible. There are lots of things I've worried about, but of course he's wonderful and I'm constantly proud of him. The tiredness does me in (he still doesn't sleep through the night) and if I had the money I'd pay a nanny lots to do night duty! But we survive.

'Sorry but no'

I have had six pregnancies and they haven't been the best of pregnancies. I thought the hospital (St James University) was very good and they do care a lot. They were very good to me with all my pregnancies and after I had each child. The money that you get off of the Social is disgusting. How they expect a woman on her own with children or child to live and feed etc., I don't know, it's like the Family Allowance, they expect you to buy clothes etc. Prices today are extremely high for children's clothes, cots, prams, school uniforms, shoes, coats, etc. The list is endless. For myself I have three children and my ex has three children. They are all our children, two boys and four girls. Now I am on my own, out of the money from the Social and Family Allowance I get I am expected to buy food, buy clothes, pay bills, buy nappies which are quite high priced, because I have tried the cheap nappies and they are no good, so you end up having to buy the dear nappies to keep your baby or small child (toddler) dry. They alone are £6 for they will last about a week but if you have more than one in nappies then you are having to pay out twice the expense. This money does not allow you for any extras.

Personally myself I find it very hard quite a lot of the time to make ends meet, especially when it comes to birthdays, Christmas and all the other things and especially if you want to take your children on holiday, etc. How the government expects a family to live off of the money we get I don't know. I always put my children first, it is on very rare occasions I can treat myself. I think they should give a little more instead of putting money up then taking out of the other hand to pay it out somewhere else, like for instance they put our money up then put the rent up so you don't really see any benefit from the rise. It's like for instance I was burgled a little while back, they practically took everything plus they trashed my home. Now I have to start again building my home up, for me and my children. I put in for a grant and a loan from the Social, they knocked me back on nearly everything which I was in real need for, like for instance because I have no heating whatsoever except the fire, a radiator I provided myself and my fire was stolen in the burglary. I borrowed a fire to keep my children warm, the Social sent some people round to have a look what I had got and what I hadn't got. Because they saw the fire they knocked me back and said I couldn't have any money to buy a fire because I have got one. I told them I had borrowed it, but they just turned round and said 'How do we know it isn't yours? You could be just saying that.'

It really makes me mad when people with families are in need of things and they ask the Social for money to buy them and they turn round and say 'Sorry, but no,' and I didn't get anything from a grant. They gave me a small amount of money on a loan, which is disgusting because I have to pay back the money off of my Social money and so much a week, so you're no better off at the end of the day and what really gets you is that the more you borrow the less you pay back a week and the less you borrow the more you have to pay back a week which I find really annoying. Because of something like this or for some other desperate reason, when you need a little help to get you through you can't get it, they tend to make it very difficult for you to cope.

I think it's very sad that families have to struggle, beg, borrow, scratch and scrape to survive in the twentieth century. The world is a very sad place I think, because they want to have a real good look and see the important things that need doing rather than all the money that's being wasted on things like making more cars – there are enough cars on the roads – and making new roads and motorways. That money, which to the imagination is quite a substantial amount of money, could be a lot better used on things which are more important. These are just a couple of examples, there are lots more, there are things more important in life than these I'm sure.

19

'I try to take each day
as it comes'

I am a 32-year-old woman who, previously to having my baby girl Karen, worked as a Homelessness Officer for the local council in Cornwall. At the same time as commencing maternity leave I moved to Brighton from Cornwall with my partner, Jonathan, as he was commencing a full-time college course. I therefore could not return to my job after having Karen, but know this would not have been my decision had I remained in Cornwall anyway. Jonathan did not continue his studies for various reasons and we therefore started to claim Income Support when my maternity benefits came to an end. The strain of bringing up a baby with no strong family support or friends on very little money whilst Jonathan was unemployed became very hard to cope with. I felt extremely alone and isolated and found that I had little energy or motivation due to the constant demands placed on me (sleepless nights with Karen became very hard to bear).

In May 1994 we made the decision, after much discussion, to live separately, and have not had a relationship since then. I found struggling financially and having Jonathan at home all the time whilst trying to raise Karen extremely difficult and now feel under less pressure for having some kind of space of my own with Karen. Jonathan continues to keep close contact with us both and this seems to work out better than before when we all lived together. He still doesn't have any work and so can be prone to depression at times. We are able to support each other better now for being able to be on our own when we need to be. We do not really have any solid reasons to be here now but I feel that since moving here in September 1993, I have made some good contacts with other mothers and would find it quite stressful to return to Cornwall at the moment and have to start again with parent-and-toddler groups, etc., as virtually all my friends down there are without children. I feel that being on Income Support with a child is very difficult as it does not allow money for any activities with them, and keeping a child amused and stimulated without many people around can be hard. However, Brighton has some brilliant facilities (both cheap and free) and this is another reason why I would hesitate to leave here.

I have thought about working but I receive at the moment £105 for my rent and £70 Income Support and Child Benefit and know that child care full-time would cost at least £70 per week. I do not feel that I would be able to get a job which would make my being away from Karen either financially or emotionally worthwhile. Even though we do not have much money I try to enjoy my time with Karen and to take each day as it comes, not looking too far ahead in the future as I feel we never know what lies ahead and it's best to make the most of the present.

Accommodation is always a worry in my mind as I have only a short-hold tenancy here and know that the landlady could decide to have the property back with very little notice. It is extremely difficult to obtain good accommodation when you have a baby, especially as most landlords ask for a month's deposit and a month's rent in advance which most families just don't have access to. This is a problem which came up time and time again in my job and causes immense strain for families who have to end up in sub-standard accommodation as they have no other choice.

20

'Despite all this we were quite a happy little family'

During the end of my pregnancy and for three months afterwards I had to survive on Income Support. This was very hard as my family was quite badly off anyway, and weren't able to help out. Luckily, my boyfriend's mother was helpful with buying clothes and necessities for the baby or I think he would have ended up sleeping in a drawer (as my first son did!). It was impossible to manage on Income Support alone without some outside help, despite the fact that I did not go out, rarely spent money on myself or anything, ate cheap meals and don't smoke. I lived in a council house which was in a bad state of repair and due for demolition (which I felt ashamed for friends to visit).

Despite all this we were quite a happy little family, and now that they are older I am able to return to college where I am presently doing a teaching degree. Although I am still in financial straits, I manage better than I did previously, partly because I have finally cleared the many debts I had from before I was on Income Support. These debts helped make it so difficult to manage on the Income Support payments which I received, as Income Support does not take previous commitments into account, but unfortunately my creditors still required regular payment (and who could blame them?). Despite this I still do not believe Income Support is sufficient to live on, even in the most basic way. Although it may be OK as a temporary measure it is too low to live on for a long period of time. I later received Family Credit as I began part-time work. Unbelievably this made me worse off despite increased incomings because they used not to take childminding payments into account (I believe this has been revised since). I was therefore working for self-esteem rather than money.

'£100 . . . to buy everything'

I have two children, my son who was born in 1987 and my daughter who was born in 1993. I am 30 years old and have just moved to this town recently from Glasgow. I don't work at the moment but I was working before I left Glasgow as a crèche worker. My partner and I have just recently split up. I received Income Support with both my son and daughter before and after they were born. With my son in 1987, I received grants for clothes for myself and a grant for baby clothes, cot, pram, etc. That money I did not have to pay back, but with my daughter in 1993, I got a grant for just £100 and that was to buy everything, clothes, cot, pram, etc. So I find it very hard now to live on Income Support with two children because now it is a loan you get from the Social Fund if anything is needed and it has to be paid back.

I can't have any more children due to health reasons but I think my two children are enough because it is very hard nowadays to bring children up on Income Support. Both my pregnancies were terrible. With both my son and daughter I spent the biggest part of my pregnancies in the hospital and both births were Caesarean sections, but I am happy with both my children. Both my children were born at Glasgow's Royal Maternity Hospital. The hospital was great and the staff, it was like a second home to me.

'Sometimes I just long to go out and enjoy a serious bout of consumerism!'

I am 33 years old and have arthritis and ankylosing spondylitis. I have a twelve-year-old daughter, an eight-month-old baby and I am a single parent. I receive Income Support and Disability Living Allowance.

I became pregnant when my medication was changed and caused my contraceptives to fail. Unfortunately this coincided with the end of the relationship I was in. However I was so delighted to be pregnant and I could not see too many problems, having brought up my daughter single-handed. I was shocked by the reactions of people close to me who assumed I would automatically have a termination, 'Surely they won't allow you to have a baby?' being a common reaction, the 'they' referring to my consultants at the hospital as if my disability was the guiding force in my life. I stopped all medication as I found it very difficult to get a straight answer from my doctors. This became more pronounced as my pregnancy progressed – no one could tell me about my condition and my pregnancy and when I asked how the maternity unit had dealt with other disabled mums I was told they had not had any other mums with mobility problems.

Fortunately I have never been backwards at coming forward and I found that if I shouted loudly enough I received help and reassurance. Near the end of my pregnancy I was permanently on crutches and this made me very tired. I spent a lot of time making things for the baby as Christmas was getting close and money was short. I found it terribly frustrating having no one to help with shopping and housework and I spent a lot of time in tears. The hospital had mentioned that Social Services may be able to help but to date I have still heard nothing. I was fitted with a TENS [Transcutaneous Electric Nerve Stimulation] machine for pain relief but the pain was so bad that three weeks before my due date I was taken into hospital to be induced. I knew that I would be having the baby without a partner or friend with me but I had assumed that someone from the hospital staff would stay with me whilst I was in labour. Having examined me and decided that I would be at least twelve hours in spite of the fact that I was insisting that I was having the baby, I was heavily sedated and put in a side room. Unfortunately I was on my back so I couldn't move or reach the call button and I was found after my waters had broken and as the baby's head was crowning.

I still have nightmares about the birth and would not want anyone to ever go through the same experience. In fact I gave birth two hours after I had been told it would not be until the next morning. James weighed in at 8 lb. 2 oz. and after being stitched I was left to get my own shower and wander back to the ward pushing James in his 'fishbowl'. We stayed in hospital for two days and when we got home it all seemed so overwhelming that Lucy (my daughter) and I just sat down and cried. I have to say that at times it has been hard but absolutely worth it. I have no help except from Lucy but we manage really well. The only negative is other people's attitudes. All those who criticized me for working when Lucy was small now take the opposite stance and insist that I am a dole scrounger because I do not work in a paid capacity. I say that when they help me I will listen, but it seems it will always be a no-win situation for single parents, especially with all the media criticism. The staff at my health centre are wonderful and as long as the children are happy and healthy then everything is OK by me! Since having James I have developed Carpel Tunnel Syndrome and I am unable to have an operation as there is no one to take care of the children. I am hoping that the splints I have been fitted with will ease the symptoms.

I think the most difficult thing about living on benefit is that you never have just enough money for anything. I am fortunate in that I don't drink or smoke, or have any social life of an evening, so I have more money than other people in a similar situation to myself, but I do get very lonely and it is hard not having another adult to discuss your problems with.

I find I have enough money to buy essential items from day to day as long as I shop carefully. I wait until the end of the day at the supermarket when fresh foods are reduced to less than half price, I go to the market for my fruit and vegetables, again at the end of the day everything is cheaper. Dry goods are never brand names, shopping carefully is a way of life now.

Clothes are more of a problem. I make most of the clothes that the baby and I wear, but having a teenage daughter and knowing how sensitive peer pressure can make a person, this is the hardest situation to deal with. I cannot afford to buy the clothes she wants, indeed trainers cost more money to buy than I get a week and this makes for most of the arguments we have. Fortunately I am quite handy with a needle and many of the shops will offload 'damaged' stock at ludicrous prices, however with very little choice. I have not had any new clothes since I was pregnant and the baby is now ten months old. Most of his clothes are handed down as they grow so quickly at this age. All his bedding and blankets are handmade but very warm and cosy. In fact the patch-work pram quilts are a great trading item and cost nothing to make except time and work.

Trading or bartering is a great way of surviving I have found, but contacting other people is sometimes difficult. As I say I make and recycle almost anything and everything, which is so politically correct these days that my daughter's friends think I choose to live like this which means she does not get so tormented about our lifestyle.

People are very quick to make judgements about someone in my situation, especially with all the media hype about single mothers, and this causes most of my attacks of the 'blues'. I have the added disadvantage of being disabled in the opinion of our glorious leaders, but the media has a huge effect on the way people react to others. However pressurized I become I would still not leave my children to go out to work. It isn't easy living like this but it does have its brighter moments and I remember a few years ago the unemployed came in for all the criticism so I shall just wait for the storm to blow over.

At this time of year I always wish for a bit more money and yet I start making all the Christmas presents about three months before and if you really think about who you are making the gift for it becomes more exciting and special. Christmas becomes more of a traditional celebration although sometimes I just long to go out and enjoy a serious bout of consumerism! Oh well, we all must have a dream . . .

23

'It is too cold a flat'

I came to England from Zaire as a refugee. It was easy to get to the antenatal clinic as they were nearby. I found that Income Support was insufficient. There was enough money for food but there is not enough to buy even clothes against the cold and we come from Zaire. I did not have enough money for gas heating, water heating and housing rent. I sent the bills to the DSS [Department of Social Security] as I cannot afford to pay them. It is too cold a flat to bring my twins home to. There has been a problem getting money from the DSS. They sent a cheque to the post office but when my husband went to collect it because I was ill they tore the cheque up. The staff at the post office said to him that your wife has to come and collect it and they destroyed it.

(Translated from French by the midwife attending this mother.)

24

'We may manage Christmas without a loan'

When I arrived home this first time, I was a bit nervous when I realized I was totally responsible for this tiny person's needs. I had no friends or family living nearby and I felt very isolated. After buying groceries, nappies and paying bills, there wasn't enough money to visit my mum. Mum was really great, she used to bring me biscuits and other little treats I couldn't afford myself, even though she was on benefits herself. Four years on and with a lot more to be thankful for, I brought my second baby son home. We had moved home since then to another flat not far away, and life had been a bit better because I had been working until I was five months pregnant.

Life with my husband has not been an easy one as he is an alcoholic. He doesn't drink every day, only when he has money in his pockets, which isn't all that often on a giro, but still it is too much. We have done without a lot because of it, and when it's been really bad he has even sold things from the house. To date he has sold three videos, two TVs, a microwave, fire and surround, Sega system, ornaments and more. It has got to the point where we do not have a video any more, or ornaments. There seems little point as it won't be there too long. For all his failings though, John is a good dad to the children and a great husband when he's sober which is most of the time because he can't afford to drink any more. At least our food has improved since we have money to buy fresh food and vegetables with the Family Credit money we get.

All my life has been a struggle. My dad seldom gave mum his wages and I have many memories of being cold and hungry and walking miles, literally, to get his wages on pay day. I know it sounds melodramatic but that's how it was. It was much the same when mum remarried as my stepdad was unemployed. I hope my children don't grow up with the same memories.

Now years on, I have two lovely children of which I am very proud. Unfortunately we are now living on benefits and it's not easy. My husband and I had just moved when I found I was pregnant so we returned home with no money and nowhere to live. I moved home to my parents and John to a friend's bedsit where I later joined him. Soon after, when I was six months pregnant, we were given a council flat. It was in a dreadful state, no wallpaper, tiles hanging off, walls drawn over with felt pens and human excrement smears on the walls and blocking the toilets. We had no money, no furniture, but luckily John's grandparents gave us a bed, TV and Belling cooker, so that made life more bearable. It wasn't just the material things, I was continually sick and had backache for my entire pregnancy and was the same four years later when I had my son.

Neither of the births were exactly positive. The children were born in different hospitals but the births were almost a carbon copy of each other. The cord was wrapped around the baby's neck and with every contraction the baby was choking. Jane was fine but Liam was rushed away for oxygen. I needed stitches on both occasions and was taken to the theatre the second time for many more stitches. Eight months on and we now live in a brand new three-bedroom house in a new estate built by the local housing association. Of course, we're now back to the frozen food, stuck in the house most of the fortnight and few visits outside, but I've learned how to budget the grocery bill a bit better. Also this year I think we may manage Christmas without a loan to pay for it, and so we might finally be out of debt for the first time in years. This is in stark contrast to previous years. I had to take out loans from companies which charge extortionate rates of interest which took the whole year to pay off, so you're back to square one. We've also had trouble with rent arrears since we first went on benefits because we hadn't filled in the proper forms. It's taken us four years to pay off our debt and at last I think we've got out of the cycle. At last I can safely let my daughter out to play. I have somewhere to hang the laundry, put the baby out in the summer and a house to relax in, instead of living in dark boxes in a stair with no daylight. Just having a garden is a real therapy.

Life with our son has been a two-sided coin, with visits to and from hospital. He developed a small bruise on his face when he was about five weeks old. In the next month it turned into an ever-growing birthmark on the left cheek. He has two types of lesions, one of which is the typical strawberry mark and the other is a fleshy raised part which extends from his nose to the opposite side of his eye. He has had three laser treatments and injections into the raised part to prevent problems with his sight, but treatment has been suspended until the mark settles. It hasn't always been easy to ignore the accusing stares and remarks made by people. At first I felt I had to explain myself to them. Now I don't, unless another child asks or someone actually asks me what the marks are.

Even with these disfiguring marks there is no disguising the good-looking wee boy with a smile that outshines any mark. I used to see the mark first, now I just see the smile. I know how lucky I am to have two such happy, contented and, so far, well-behaved children who love each other to bits, and give us a lot of fun and exhaustion!

25

'I think it's not right what they do with the Travelling people'

We know what eviction is like, like that they're going to come around at six o'clock in the morning but it's the children, they don't know. Because they lie on in the winter and you tell them they're going to get evicted in the morning but they don't realize what's going to happen.

The time it happened in North Street, that was when my sister was pregnant. Her husband was away and she was about six—seven months pregnant but they came and started evicting us early in the morning. She was getting ready then, when she got up the children were screaming, hysterical because it was a very winter's morning and it was teeming rain as well. So they went over to the trailers, hers was the first trailer they went to. She was very upset, her nerves were at her over her husband being away and she was having a child and everything.

'Just wait' she said 'till I give the children something to eat and I dress them', but no way would they even give her a chance so she ran out. They started pulling up the caravan, trying to drag it. But she went back and she wouldn't come out so they started pulling out the trailer with her and the children in it and if anything had fallen anything could have happened to her at that time.

I think it's not right what they do with the Travelling people. When we all moved into this big camp, they tipped in a whole load of skips of rubbish at the gate, so we couldn't get in or out. It was in the middle of winter, it was terrible, the camp was scruffy, dirty, there were no toilets, no nothing on it. You know, you can imagine when you're pregnant and you want to go to the toilet and there's nowhere to go, because all the trailers are all together and everyone is looking at you and you have to go miles to get to a toilet.

We were there about a week and we used to climb over all the muck, and I was pregnant at the time with Mary. Then one night, about two weeks after, I went into labour and there was no way that we could get out to get the ambulance. It was about a mile down the road to the phone, so Bill had to go across all the fields to phone an ambulance.

But when the ambulance came to take me to the hospital there was no way they could drive the ambulance in. So what they had to do, they had to come over all this big pile of muck where they had to climb right up to the top of it and then come down the other side. When they came into the trailer they looked at me, they examined me, and they knew that I was ready to have the baby any time. Now there was no way they could get the ambulance in to get me out. So I had to pack my things and walk all the way back out, climb over all the muck myself, back down the other side and into the ambulance. When I got to the hospital I was covered over in muck. But next day Bill came up to see me in the hospital and he told me that the bulldozer came down to take away all the muck off away from the camp.

I was only three days in hospital and when I came back we had to move to this other camp. The police would just come right behind us and they'd tell us to move. They'd keep following us out along the motorway till we got so many miles out and they'd leave us back there then. We'd have to come back then and look for another camp and this was going on for three days, maybe twelve or one o'clock at night, we were getting shifted. The child wasn't getting any bottles, we didn't have any gas or anything.

26

'My friend's family have taken me under their wing'

My first son was born in April 1991, I returned to work when he was three months old. All went well, a close friend looked after him and everything was great. My second son was born in March 1995. My plans were basically the same as they had been the first time but nothing quite went to plan. I was fortunate to have the support of a terrific health visitor and GP when I realized I was suffering from postnatal depression. I was also diagnosed in July 1995 as suffering from multiple sclerosis. The combination of both was almost unbearable. However, as I mentioned, my health visitor and GP were great. I felt well cared for and didn't even have to ask for help, they were there, offering it and making sure that I was coping. I was also lucky to be cared for by my best friend's mother. My own mother died when I was a child, so much of the news I had to cope with last year was not shared with parents. My friend's family have taken me under their wing, treating me like another daughter. They have turned up at all hours of the day and night in response to my telephone calls, asking for help. I will be forever indebted to them all. My children simply think of them as grandparents.

Slowly I managed to get back to some kind of normality and returned to full-time work in December when the baby was almost nine months old. On this occasion I would happily have remained at home to look after my children but, like most mothers who work, I do so because I have to and not because I want to. My husband and I both work in basic-grade clerical posts with the local authority, so we don't have large salaries. One thing I would love to see more of is workplace crèches. I work in a school and believe that it would be fairly easy for staff with children to employ nursery nurses to look after children within the child-centred environment that already exists. I am at present trying to decide if I can afford to reduce my working hours in order to spend more time with the children and at the same time maintain my health as much as possible. I am fortunate to also have a wonderful husband who supports me at all times and who idolizes his two sons.

I feel that at my age (32), having been married for eleven years, having a fairly secure job, my own home, car, etc., having a family seemed like a natural progression which should have been fairly undramatic. Not so. I admire so much single mothers with little family support who manage to work. How do they do it?

'My claim for Income Support'

I am 38 and have three children aged twelve, nine and three. My husband is 42 this year and has accountancy qualifications and is a Citizen's Advice Bureau (CAB) adviser. I have training in child care and crèche work. I would like you to know that when I applied for a Maternity Grant I was refused because I was only on Income Support for two days. If I had enclosed the Maternity Grant claim form with my claim for Income Support I would have got it.

We were very happy with the hospital care and the health visitor when the baby was born.

Many people don't realize they qualify for Income Support as their benefit is delayed (the increase for the child) while their benefit books are amended. In our case Income Support was payable for two days and was applied for, but a Maternity Grant form was sent to the DSS [Department of Social Security] after the Income Support had expired. There was only a few days delay in sending in the Maternity Grant form but as we were not now on Income Support we did not qualify for it. My husband had only just joined the CAB and so was not aware of what to do in the situation.

'I had to walk twelve miles round trip to the hospital'

I have five children. When I was having David, he is my second child, I was at my poorest. I was living in a small flat with my oldest son, my husband and his father, who at the time had nowhere to live. I was pregnant and under a lot of stress. Matthew, my eldest, was out playing when a man from the shop came and told me he had had an accident on the railway. A train had hit his leg. I ran to the railway line but the police wouldn't let me go up to him, he was in a bad way. I found out later his leg was hanging out, they told me at the hospital. The shock was terrible and I had the baby early because of it. Money was very short, we put David in a large drawer, we couldn't afford a cot. Any money we had went on food and clothes for the baby, they were mostly secondhand and I was tired trying to make ends meet. Often I was confused.

When Matthew had to have the rest of his leg taken off, it took me six hours to sign the papers. I was on my own, except for Matthew's friend and the police. I didn't want him to have his leg off but in the end I did sign, I had no choice. Things got worse because I had a new baby and no money. Visiting Matthew in hospital was hard because I had no bus fare. I did have help from the community centre. They had a collection. Help was also given with pyjamas and a dressing gown out of the club. I never missed a visit. Sometimes I had to walk twelve miles round trip to the hospital. I walked alone at 10 o'clock at night. One day Matthew was transferred to have his leg measured. When I had walked to the hospital I was late and had missed him. Feeling helpless I cried not knowing what to do, my son was alone and I wanted to be with him. The ambulance driver understood and gave me my train fare to get to Birmingham. I was relieved. My only thought was to get to him. When I did arrive I must have looked bad because the nurse gave me a cup of tea and said sit down. I had no idea how I was going to get home but in the end the ambulance took me with Matthew.

When Matthew came home the flat was overcrowded and I couldn't lift him up and down the stairs, so he went to my mum's. In the June after the baby was born I suffered from postnatal depression. This meant I couldn't cope. My sister had to come and help me during the day. While she was doing this I went to see Matthew. My husband was no help at all. We were having lots of problems. He couldn't get a job and we argued about money all the time. It was really bad times. I sometimes think how did we survive? I now have three more children and we are still married but not without problems. Life would have been much easier had I had the right help.

29

'Statutory Maternity Pay barely got the groceries'

My husband, John, worked for his father as a farm labourer and I was unemployed when we met, then I got a part-time job working as a care assistant in an old people's home. We were having money to go out one or two nights per week at the local bar, then John proposed and so I looked for another job. Luckily I found one as a stitcher in the local factory. John was working nights in a part-time job from 7 p.m. to 3 a.m. His part-time job was paying to keep and run the car. I was working seven days a week from March until September to pay for the wedding. We couldn't afford to go out. We had no social life but if we were to go out it would be to a friend's house. Each week I paid a bit off my dress, the bridesmaids' dresses, the flowers, the cars . . . if I had any money left I bought cigarettes, washing-up liquid, washing powder or something for the house in September. I had a lot of knick-knacks for the house we were to be in when we got married, but in September I found out that I was pregnant. I knew I had to slow down and so I gave up my job working Saturday and Sunday in the old people's home. The wedding was nearly paid for but my health was also paying its price, I was forever getting infections – chest, urine, and I was under a lot of stress being pregnant and no one knowing. The stress of the wedding, everything.

On 17 November we got married and with money we received as wedding gifts we could afford four days in Scotland. We came home on Monday and on the Tuesday I went for my first antenatal class and that night we told everybody that I was three months pregnant. After we got married I had to move in with John's parents as the builders were not finished. It was a nightmare. My mother and father had paid for the rest of the wedding and if they hadn't, we couldn't have afforded it. John's parents wouldn't take any money for our keep so I bought some groceries just to help out. Every week I left money aside to buy more things for my house. John received £50 from his work with his father and it kept petrol in the car to take me to the factory and back. We were literally living on people's good nature. I earned £75 a week from working in the factory and it was tough saving for Christmas presents and getting things for the house. It wasn't easy, Christmas came and went and still no house. By March the stress of living with my in-laws, they wouldn't give me my privacy, they walked in and out of the bedroom, they were forever interfering in our business and as well as being pregnant, I was under a lot of stress. It was the worst time of my life.

Finally on 17 March our house was finished, so we moved in with all the stuff I had bought for the house. I didn't need much for the kitchen, our living room was completely furnished, our bedroom was well under way and we only needed carpet, paint or wallpaper or beds, wardrobes . . . As soon as we moved in, every week we bought things for the baby, car seat, bibs, vest, babygrows . . . John then had to leave working for his father and got a full-time job to pay the mortgage, rates, electricity. Also in March I had to go off on maternity leave. My depression was getting worse and my grandfather died which set me back again. We were living on John's pay as my Statutory Maternity Pay barely got the groceries.

In May Amy was born and money was very tight, my Statutory Maternity Pay wasn't getting us food never mind a newborn baby. Again we had to dip into the little savings we had. With John running to the hospital twice a day to visit us petrol was becoming a daily requirement. If I asked John to bring me in anything, that was more money. In the hospital we had to provide everything for the baby and ourselves, the only thing that was free was the baby's milk. To be honest it would have been better in the years of cutbacks. For the future I would like to see nappies, pads and breastpads all supplied or at least cheaper in the hospital (maternity wings) rather than shops or chemists. I was told to bring in a bag of towels or a packet but I had to keep sending John out for more. Again more money – it was all adding up. I couldn't wait to see how John was getting on at home and I wanted to be there for him. He was having to buy food for himself at home and try and get to work. Ideally I would love to see a law going through that fathers would be allowed time off work with pay when their partners are in having babies and to be there when the baby's home for a week or two after.

Luckily I got out on a Sunday and John did not have to work. After my maternity pay was finished I was still on anti-depressants and was faced with going back to work, paying for a babysitter and not feeling up to it or going on the sick, getting in touch with myself, trying to live every day and trying to get better but having hardly any money coming in. I decided to stay off and my doctor and I felt that if I did go back to work it might make things worse. Most importantly I didn't want to be away from my baby, she was the one thing I was living for and John knew it. The postnatal depression was getting worse and worse and I felt I was sliding into a hole. I kept on thinking of a film I'd seen on TV when a family was telling their daughter to go towards the light. Well for me there was no light and I was being turned back not forward. There was no money and, as I thought, no point. I was living for Amy and nothing or no one else. John and I became strained, I couldn't wait for him to get home at night but as soon as he came in through the door I ate the head off him for the slightest wee thing. Suddenly we were in debt to the bank and John and the bank decided to call it a loan. No money on my side coming in and John's pay was to pay all the bills and now to pay back the loan. We had no other choice. I had to either find a job that paid more or go back to my old one, but one way or another I had to go back. Luckily within a month I had found one and started back to work. I was out of the repetitive factory work and had got a job in an old people's home. That was back in October.

We are still struggling with money, paying the bills. We cannot afford a social life but I can afford the groceries. The money which John paid the groceries with goes on to paying the loan. Next month the tax, MOT and insurance are due on the car and we do not know where the money is going to come from. The only good thing I've been able to do is get off the anti-depressants. I'm still not sleeping at night, I don't know whether it's to do with postnatal depression or money worries. John and myself are getting on a bit better since I started my relief post as a care assistant but it's still hard. When I returned to work my mother said she would look after Amy for nothing until such time when our financial position got better. If it wasn't for my mother we couldn't afford to eat. The only good note I'll end with is this, there are two full-time posts coming up at the end of the month in work and I've got my application form in. It will be a steady and better income than what I'm getting now. I just pray that I get it and get out of this hole my little family is in or I don't know what will happen.

'Rising damp'

I was eighteen when I found out I was pregnant. For the first three months I was permanently ill due to changing hormones (morning sickness). As a result I was forced to drop out of my college course (beauty therapy). Fearing lots of flak from both sets of parents we decided to move out and try to set up a home of our own. The house wasn't much, but it was ours, and we were together and that was all that mattered or so we thought. My boyfriend Tony was serving an apprenticeship as an engineer and wasn't well paid. We could barely afford to eat, as I wasn't entitled to any benefits through my boyfriend committing the ultimate crime and working.

The house was a shambles, it had rising damp and old electrics. Every day revealed a new flaw in our love nest. Both sets of parents helped out whenever they could, they offered to put us up for the night to get away from 'that' house. But we declined their offers because we feared the only luxuries we actually owned, i.e., portable TV, stereo, etc., would be stolen through someone burglaring our property. The area the house was in wasn't very desirable to say the least. Two or three doors down the street lived one of the main crooks in this town. He had crews of young lads scouting round looking for houses to burgle. These young lads often looked in our windows, checking out what 'goodies' we had, when my boyfriend was at work. This understandably made us very uncomfortable because we weren't able to say or do anything to avoid any trouble, because of being strangers in the area. The landlord started becoming shirty when we asked him to sort out the rising damp and various other faults, because my health was beginning to ail. He took my boyfriend into the back room of his pub, where no one could see, and started hurling obscenities and making threats of bodily violence. He was an extremely large 'navvy' type person. This was the final straw. That day my boyfriend decided to do a 'midnight flit'. We had paid one week's rent as deposit. We used that up and moved out. Tony's cousin arranged a transit pick-up van and we loaded all our stuff on it and drove back to my boyfriend's house. We must have looked like the Beverly Hillbillies driving through the back streets. We even had two cats sat in the cab.

When we moved back to my boyfriend's parents' house, which was four miles away on the outskirts of town, in a very nice area, they could only put us up on an airbed in the front room of their two-up, two-down terraced house, not that we were complaining. There are Tony's parents, his younger brother (who is fourteen), a dog and three cats (who are mad as hatters) and us. Now and again tempers get a bit frayed and arguments do occur. But on the whole we do get on fine.

His parents take a bit of board off us. We pay half the rent and buy half the food. Towards the end of my pregnancy I had to visit the doctor's once a week for a check-up, because I had slightly high blood pressure. At the last check-up I went to, the doctor tested my water sample and detected protein in it. He tested my blood pressure and noticed that it was very high. He told me to get to hospital as soon as possible because he thought I might be developing pre-eclampsia and I could lose the baby. I rushed back to the house and rang my dad to organize a lift. I then rang my boyfriend at work, who came home at once.

I went into hospital quite unprepared. I had a bag packed but we didn't have everything we needed. The hospital told me not to worry as I would probably be going home tomorrow. My dad stayed for about an hour and Tony stayed till eight o'clock that evening. Just before he left he nipped across the road and treated me to a Kentucky Fried Chicken slap-up meal.

At about ten o'clock I went for a bath and went to bed. All of a sudden I felt something strange, then my waters broke. I called for the nurse, who asked me if I'd had contractions, but I hadn't and I didn't get them until half an hour after my waters broke. They rang Tony at about twelve o'clock (Tony said it was about 12.03, because he couldn't forget that phone call!). The conversation they had went: 'Hello, is that Tony?' 'Yeah' (still half asleep). 'It's the hospital, we think, Valerie is going into labour.' 'Oh God,' replied Tony. 'Is she alright?' 'Yes,' the nurse reassured Tony. 'Tell her to hold on, I'll be there as soon as possible.'

Meanwhile I was having contractions every two minutes. Tony arrived in a taxi, they showed him in, I was bent over in the middle of a contraction, huffing and puffing. When Tony saw me, all he said was 'Oh dear,' which is unusual for him as he is usually quite graphic. Once the contraction stopped I started to pack my bag, the nurses said 'Don't bother.' Tony tried to help but he was shaking too much. They convinced me to leave my bag and go to the labour ward upstairs. I had to stop halfway up the stairs as I had a contraction for two or three minutes! In the delivery room I told the midwife I want half a dose of pethidine and gas and air. I had always said I only wanted gas and air but the pain was too bad. After a few hours of pushing and breathing I had a little boy. When he was born they put him on my chest. I commented 'Oh, he's lovely. It wasn't that bad, we can have some more'!

Tony nearly fainted. We named him William. Tony held him while the midwife tended to me. I went for a bath while the midwife checked out William's reactions, lungs, etc. He started crying two minutes after I went out of the room. Tony tried tending to him but didn't know what to do. I was taken back on to the ward shattered. But I didn't get any sleep, I was too excited! Tony and all the relations came to visit me and William, bearing gifts and flowers, everyone was close to tears.

I came home four days later and for weeks had many sleepless nights. Fortunately Tony's boss (who is his uncle) let him off work for two weeks. William is now nine weeks old, and just had his first immunizations, I nearly broke my heart because he was screaming that much. We are still sleeping on the airbed, with no sign of a house in the foreseeable future. Not even off the council. But we are sure people have had to struggle through worse circumstances. All we have to do is just struggle on regardless. As all comes to he who waits.

31

'I hate being on the DSS, I want to work'

I am a 25-year-old single parent of two children. Money problems: I receive Income Support of £57.19 per week and Child Benefit/ One-Parent Benefit of £25.30 per week. This money is supposed to feed, clothe and pay bills, but it goes nowhere. I struggle by each week on this. I have been offered jobs in full-time employment, which is what I want, but when I work out child-care costs, paying my rent, council tax, etc., I'm no better off. I hate being on the DSS [Department of Social Security], I want to work. I'm clever and I hate being in the mess I'm in. The government say that young girls get pregnant to get a house. I didn't, I had one. But to any girl who's thinking of getting pregnant to keep their boyfriend or get a council house I'd tell them not to be so stupid, think first.

Relationships: I was nineteen when I had my first child and it wasn't easy and it never will be. I'd been with my son's father for three years. In 1991 I had a daughter, when we split up. He (that's my boyfriend) went to live with my sister over the road from me. I found life getting harder and harder by the day. Over the years I've grown up and grown tougher. I think now I can survive almost anything. This affected my son badly and now he stays with his father and my sister and their children, while I've moved to the next village with my daughter who's five. The family think I'm cruel moving house and leaving my son, but if I'd have carried on living there I would not have been able to get on with my life. I wish things could have been different. Don't get me wrong, I would never go back to my children's father. I stopped loving him in 1991. I have a fantastic boyfriend now who I love to bits and I've been with him for fourteen months. My daughter loves him but my son won't show us how he feels. I wish I'd met the man I'm with now when I was sixteen because I can honestly say he's the right one.

'"Lowering the tone"
of the school'

I am twenty years old, married with two children. I was seventeen when I gave birth to my oldest child, Roger. When I first found out I was pregnant, I was really pleased, but my Dad did not speak to me for almost seven months and my Mum pretended it was not happening. I was still at school studying for my A levels. At six months pregnant I was asked not so politely to leave as I was 'lowering the tone' of the school. My parents think the sun shines out of my son's behind!

I was treated like a leper by my doctor and community midwife. My health visitor assumed I couldn't cope, she was newly qualified with no children – I saw her once. The general response was disgust, embarrassment, patronizing attitudes. The birth was 34 hours of hell. I was not told what was happening or asked what I wanted. The parentcraft classes were a nightmare geared specifically for older parents. Legendary council houses did not appear and I had no money until three weeks after Roger was born and that was a 'bridging payment' to last another nine-and-a-half weeks! Boy was I skint! I joined the Campaign for Young Parents which challenges all the attitudes above and tries to prevent other parents having the difficulties I've had.

I was a lucky one, I had a man to stand by me, a family who reluctantly let me stay at home and a beautiful son who I desperately wanted, loved and cared for, and now a daughter, Lucy, to join him!

'I just wish I had £10 to spend on anything I wanted'

When I first left work, seven weeks prior to my daughter's birth, it was not too bad because I was receiving 90 per cent of my average pay in the first six weeks, but when it was reduced to £50-plus, life became very difficult and we found it hard to meet the bills. We have outgoings of £600 per month and then have to buy food and clothing and need money for gas and electricity. My husband is self-employed, some weeks earning lots of money, some weeks hardly anything. We dread any unforeseen expenditure, especially if the car breaks down, because then we have to choose whether to have it mended or pay the mortgage (we have to have it repaired because my husband can't work unless he has transport). We are constantly worried. My husband feels he can't support us as 'a man should' and sometimes I feel irritated that he's not got a 'proper job' with a regular wage. Sometimes he works from 8 a.m. to 10 p.m. at night. Alternate weeks he works until 2 p.m., then I work 2 p.m. to 11 p.m. The second week my mother-in-law has the baby so we both work. He works during the day, and I work from 2 p.m. to 11 p.m.

We live in a small one-bedroomed flat. The baby has the bedroom and we sleep in the living room. We bought the house when the Conservatives kept on about home ownership and now we have £10,000 negative equity, so can't see ourselves ever moving. We are always anxious about providing enough for the baby. We never buy clothes. The baby is clothed by grandparents and family. We never go out and never go on holiday. Our last holiday was over four years ago, a week in Skegness. My husband is always asleep when I get in from work at 11.30 p.m. Last week the car broke down and my husband had to walk for four hours because he couldn't afford to catch a bus or any transport. I just wish I had £10 to spend on anything I wanted.

'When my husband became a full-time student we lost all benefits'

When I was pregnant with my first child, I was a single parent living on my own. This was in 1987. I was receiving Income Support. When I got my house I was given a grant of £150 to buy a cooker, £40 to carpet and decorate. I also received £80 Maternity Payment, which was one payment only, and a single bed and bedding from the DSS [Department of Social Security]. I also had the opportunity to apply for money for clothes and footwear for myself and to buy a cot, highchair and babygate for the stairs as I lived in a block of flats.

In 1991 I gave birth to my second child. At the time of birth my husband was claiming Income Support. The grant system had been replaced by a loan system which had to be paid back. Fortunately I had kept the essentials from my first child, i.e., the cot and bedding, sterilizing unit and baby bath, because we could not afford to borrow the money to buy these things.

I was entitled to free milk for the baby and my daughter received free school meals. But when my husband became a full-time student, earning £15 per week less than on Income Support, we lost all benefits, including free milk and free school meals and had to pay a percentage towards our rent charges.

'I can't relax or see anything in the future'

I had my daughter, Lee, in 1993. It was a very quick birth and the midwife I had, my husband and I felt, rushed the final stage, and I was very concerned I was bleeding so heavily. The midwife did not seem to think it was a problem and I was back on a ward within quarter of an hour of having Lee (still bleeding heavily). I then heard her say to the Sister on duty to keep an eye on me as I had lost about 300 ml. of blood. This worried me more and the next day I had blood clots the size of a big man's hand coming from me, but was still assured everything was alright. I went home the following day feeling exhausted and fragile which I never did with my first daughter, Josie. The whole week I continued to bleed heavily and lose big blood clots, but was assured this was normal. I stopped worrying until about three weeks later. We were going to my mum and dad's and as I got out of the car I suddenly felt as though I was bleeding heavily. We got up to my mum's house and she made me go to the toilet (at this stage I was shaking with fear). She held my hand as I inspected what was going on, and I passed three blood clots. A few days later the same thing happened again, but this time I had blood gushing from me also. I was terrified and went to see my doctor at the medical centre who immediately made an urgent appointment for me to have a D & C [Dilation & Curettage – a surgical 'scrape'] the next day. By the morning I was so frightened I couldn't even stand up as I was just pouring with blood and clots. My husband rang our doctor who came straight away and he took one look at me and sent for an ambulance right away. I arrived at the hospital feeling drained and very frightened. I had a D & C done and the doctor on duty the next day told me I still had a large amount of placenta left inside me. I was just so relieved it was over with, or so I thought. I came home the next day and about four days later I was in agony in my womb area. By the end of that week my doctor sent me to hospital to have intravenous antibiotics. I was in there just two days and sent home feeling very sick. I knew I still was unwell. Luckily my mum was able to look after my two girls and me when I got home. The pain didn't ease up though and nine days later, my doctor sent me by ambulance, again, to hospital. This time they took it more seriously and I had intravenous antibiotics for a week, but then I started getting panic attacks and they sent me home with a district nurse coming twice a day to give me antibiotics by injection. I got myself in such a state my doctor put me on beta blockers as my pulse was constantly around 130 beats per minute. All I had was flashbacks to the trauma I had been through and the pain still didn't ease until I had a laparoscopy in the July after. Then the pain stopped. After all I had been through, depression set in very badly and I seriously considered suicide. My doctor wanted me to go into a psychiatric hospital, but I refused, I am terrified of hospitals now. My health visitor was so good to me and my doctor, I don't know what I would have done without them. I was put on anti-depressants, which I am still on over two years later and valium and sleeping tablets. To make matters worse, at the time my mum wouldn't accept I had depression and told me to 'pull myself together'. This eventually led to my husband having a huge argument with her and we didn't speak for weeks. I started to see a psychiatric nurse who suggested a meeting with him, me, my mum and a consultant psychiatrist. Even though it helped a bit, it really will never be the same between us again.

I have since been diagnosed as having 'post traumatic stress disorder' and cannot relax or see anything in the future to look forward to. It has stopped my part-time hairdressing and because my husband's wage is just above (about £45 over) our entitlement for Family Credit, we do find it hard to make ends meet. With prescriptions at £5.25 a go, you can imagine how much I spend on them. It leaves me feeling very bitter towards my health authority and many people have advised me to take legal action, but I just feel I cannot go through any more. I would just like to take this opportunity to say that without my lovely health visitor and doctor I really don't think I would be here now. They have been a tower of strength and I can never thank them enough, it's just a shame the health authority could not be the same.

36

'But it has to do'

The doctors and my midwife were so helpful I could not ask for more, and I got a Maternity Grant to buy my child's clothes and it was not a lot but it had to do. It just got the things I needed. My income I have to live on, that was not a lot of money for myself and my two children but it had to do. Still I've still not got a lot, but it has to do.

37

'I lived in one room with no electric points in the room, no windows'

I am a working mother of three children. My children are now aged twenty-two, twenty and twelve years. I was seventeen years of age when I become pregnant with my daughter. I was a copy typist working in the City. I was also unmarried. I felt stigmatized and hid my pregnancy from my employers. I experienced a terrible pregnancy, but had no one to turn to except my two older sisters who were also very young. The father of my two eldest children was in prison at the time, I therefore had no additional financial support. When I eventually gave up work, I was seven months pregnant. My employers still did not know I was pregnant, I was terrified to tell them as I thought they would sack me! Looking back now, when I wrote to them and told them I would not be coming back because of my pregnancy, they were very supportive. They sent me a card and baby clothes! I had never lived on benefits before, and did I suffer!! I did not know my true entitlements and the information was not easily accessible. I lived in one room with no electric points in the room, no windows for ventilation. I lived there until my second child was born. He became very ill from poor housing conditions. When he was three months he spent the next three months in hospital. I thought he was going to die as he had breathing difficulties and kept going blue in his face. This was directly related to our home conditions. I had to fight with the authorities to receive adequate housing.

My third child did not suffer from lack of money or poor housing conditions like his elder brother and sister. His father cares about all of my children and me. With his support I have pursued my career and I now work assisting people in an advisory capacity. I can relate to the problems other mothers experience. I have been there. I know there is light at the end of the tunnel. There are more advice agencies available to inform people of their entitlements. Pity the housing and benefits agencies do not see this as a priority!

38

'The DSS have been a godsend'

I am 38 years young, have two daughters, aged seven and nine, with a third due on 28 March. Yes, I know it's a girl due to the wonders of modern science, which incidentally has helped my decisions on the future. I am a one-parent family, not by choice, but my 'ex' no longer wanted the 'responsibility of a wife, children and mortgage', and 'wanted a new life' (his words – not mine!). To put it bluntly, I struggled emotionally and financially at first, receiving no help from my husband and his family, who all incidentally live in the same road. They would not even look after the children while I worked extra hours to raise money. My own family live 300 miles away. So once the feeling of being totally worthless passed, the anger set in and I wanted to prove I could survive, and I have, with the help of a very good friend and her husband.

Solicitors have been no great help – after all, it's just a job to them, and the advice they offered – if you knew what you wanted – was minimal, although I must admit to becoming fairly good friends with mine. The DSS [Department of Social Security] have been a godsend, not just for help with cash, but with advice and who to contact. The same with the Child Support Agency. It has taken many months to reach the required assessments, but they have always been patient and willing to help. The family courts have behaved atrociously. When I asked for a court welfare officer to be appointed, as my children refused to see their father (due to reasons I'll explain), it was refused. I had four separate family-court appearances – twice with different judges, one who made it perfectly clear that he didn't like strong-minded women with an opinion. A court welfare officer has now been appointed and the first letter I received called me by a different Christian name and spelt my surname incorrectly!

On attempting to open a bank account at the branch where I originally had my joint account with my 'ex' – no problem, until it came to a Mastercard. I was told I wasn't entitled as the previous one had been in my husband's name with myself as the secondary cardholder. Let's just say I now eventually have one! The local borough council have generated more paperwork than I can believe, and trying to obtain information is such hard work. My council tax has been reduced, but accompanying 'decisions' need a degree in pure mathematics to decipher.

I have started to attend night school, something that I would never have done had I remained married, and have found all my local college staff more than helpful, as with my leisure centre, in obtaining reduced-rate passes due to being on low income. I was absolutely disgusted with my car insurers. I had obviously been on my husband's policy for the last x number of years – resulting in me not being eligible for a no-claims bonus. This is never pointed out or allowed for. My employers, a major retail company, I must admit, have been excellent. I originally was employed three full days, but offered to resign as I had no one to care for the children after school. They offered me a lower-paid job but working over five days within school hours, and when financially struggling they offered an interest-free loan, which I managed without. We also have a store doctor and occupational health therapist who I see regularly at no charge! The costs of being a one-parent family are obviously greater, I have to pay a childminder on Saturdays and school holidays, and sometimes convenience foods are not an option. We regularly visit car-boot and jumble sales, but I always make it into a game for the girls and they seem to enjoy the experience of 'how much we can get for how little'.

I have been intimidated by my ex-husband and his family and

they want me to move from the matrimonial home (a bad penny methinks!), to the point where I have been arrested, spent a night in cells and had all charges dismissed. The police have been no help at all. My 'ex' is a serving PC [police constable] and I have suffered nothing but harassment from them. I took the children away to family in the summer only to be told by a sergeant on returning unexpectedly, 'What have you come back for?' Although I have gone from strength to strength it has been, and is, an uphill struggle. Decisions are solely mine and you worry what would happen to the children if anything unforeseen happens to yourself. I have made financial provisions, but material things are not what really matters. That is my biggest worry. We would manage without all the material objects as long as we have each other. I must admit, I am much closer to my daughters than I have ever been. I just wish there wasn't this 'one-parent family' tag. I work, we care about the environment, we help others, we raise money through sponsorship, but as soon as you are labelled a one-parent family, people assume trouble. Also, with changing my name back to my maiden name, the bank clerk insisted he had to 'put me into a box' as regarding my marital status, e.g., Mrs, Miss or Ms. When I explained I was none of these and wanted to be plain me he became quite agitated and said 'Oh, you're one of those women are you?' To which I asked him to tick the 'Mr' box! My account is in the name I wanted. The paperwork side to being a single parent is absolutely horrendous, I have spent many hours filling in basically the same documentation for government departments. Couldn't it all be cross-referenced?

The hospital where I am due to have my baby is wonderful – no questions asked and you're treated the same as everyone else, long gone are the old 'workhouse' attitudes. I still come across people who think I (we) should put up and shut up, be seen and not heard and should put up with our lot! But life is for living – no one is going to live it for you, and you must make the best of things. Very different now I'm sure, I'm not afraid to be outspoken and stand up and be counted, and although it can still be difficult

– it can happen in today's society. Faith and belief! I'll get down off my soapbox now. Seriously, I have had some horrendous times lately, but it does get better and you must never stop questioning and asking (and form-filling!)

39

'I wouldn't swap my life with anybody'

Every time I hear about people struggling on benefit it makes me really cross. I've been on benefit for years. I have two sons of nearly nineteen and fifteen and a golden retriever. I have a pretty garden flat behind the seafront which I bought very cheap and did up myself. I am 43, slim and fit. I buy beautiful clothes from charity shops for me and new ones for the kids. I live on cabbage cooked with tinned tomatoes at 14p at Gateways. The last cabbage weighed 3.5 pounds and cost 15p. I buy meat on offer, reduced, for the kids very cheaply. Golden Delicious apples cost 22p a pound in Gateways at the moment. The last frozen chicken I bought cost me 45p a pound in Sainsburys. I have a few shares and am lending my elder son £1,500 to buy himself a motorbike.

I don't go on holidays but who wants to? The kids go to Italy to see their father in the summer and he pays. I have cleaning jobs with neighbours and make an extra £15 a week. I love going round market stalls and picking up bargains. I have loads of plants in my sitting room and bedrooms that look really pretty and last for years if watered. Most of my furniture is second-hand but it looks nice. I have a good life and enjoy myself walking the dog, shopping, watching television and gardening. I have plenty to do and wouldn't swap my life with anybody.

P.S. I make delicious home-made cakes, jam and bread.

40

'I never saw Social Services again but I thank them for the help they gave us'

I am a housewife. I have two children, a daughter twelve years of age and a boy nine years. My husband and I have been together for twenty years. I was overjoyed when I found out after seven years of trying for a child it had finally happened. We were so excited, but my excitement soon turned. Trips to hospitals and doctors were a nightmare all because of my weight. I was not a perfect size 10. Every time I went to the doctors I left in tears. I ended up not looking forward to the birth of my child, because for nine months I was told of the trouble I would have giving birth to my baby all because, as I've said, of my weight. When the time came I was so scared. Thank God I had a good labour and birth and a perfect little girl, Susan, who weighed 6 lb. 8 oz. Everything would have been great if only I didn't have to put up with all those fat comments made by the medical people. I hope this does not happen too often. I have since had a boy, Daniel. My family is now complete.

Everything was right in my life, all I ever wanted was a good and loving husband, and a beautiful daughter, and she also had everything she could possibly need, thanks to her wonderful nan Alice. My daughter was a few months old when my life fell apart. My husband decided to tell me he was having trouble keeping up with our mortgage payments plus he was behind with the payments to the gas company to the tune of £300. I was desperate. Where do I go? Who do I talk to?

One day my health visitor came to my home to do a development test on Susan. Between bouts of uncontrollable crying I explained to her my situation. I didn't expect the reply she gave me, she didn't know how to help. After she left I sat still crying and cuddling my daughter for a long period of time. With all our money worries came the inevitable breaking down in my husband's and my relationship, the arguments became more heated and more frequent. The effect on myself was devastating. I stopped going out and found I could not cope with simple tasks like shopping. A few weeks later my health visitor came back and asked me how I would feel about getting in touch with Social Services. My attitude to this was I would do anything if it would help me and my family. I delayed ringing the number she gave me until the next day. Silly things were going through my mind, the biggest one was, will they take Susan away from me? But it was the best thing I could have done.

This stranger came to my door, sat with me for what seemed like hours, writing things down every now and again. As she stood at the door her parting words to me were don't worry and she would be back in touch soon. It was maybe a week later she returned her call and presented me with a cheque for the outstanding gas bill explaining this was a one-off payment. She also arranged for a visitor to call once a week to help me get out of my house and support me through my panic attacks. It felt like the weight of the world had been lifted off my shoulders. I never saw Social Services again but I thank them for the help they gave us without intruding into our lives. It didn't solve all our problems, money was still a big issue. We ended up losing our house. However, I have a lot to be grateful for. I live in a council-owned house now, we will always have to struggle with money, never keeping our heads above water but learning to live with it.

As a mother I feel I have done my very best. My children don't always get the things in life they would like, but they do have all the love they would ever need. Now my children are older I have made changes for myself. I have become a volunteer at my local centre in an area of high unemployment and a high level of single parents and with this comes many problems. I have also ventured back into education, my first exams will be next Easter. All this has had a positive effect on me which in turn must have a positive effect on my children.

41

'Good friends give me handouts. My husband . . . would feel ashamed'

I had my first baby in 1986, second in 1989 and third in 1992. I love caring for my babies. But we are out of work. We found it hard to buy things for our kids. I had to buy second-hand prams and cots. I have some good friends who give me handouts (good clothing). My husband doesn't know. He would feel ashamed. Not me, I am very grateful. The thing that got to me when I was at home with Katy, my first, it was about the second week, I just cried, I don't know why but I did, even in the street, pushing Katy in her pram. I didn't tell anybody because I felt silly and it went on for three weeks until I told my health visitor. I talked it through with her. I'm glad I did.

But when I got Kylie, my second, I had built my hopes up for a boy through my nine months, before I gave birth. I told the nurse if it's a girl give her straight to her dad, but the nurse put some tissue on my stomach to get a bond with Kylie. She knew by the look on my face I was upset it was a girl. I kept telling myself she is beautiful, love her, but I couldn't. I would feed her at arm's length, then the nurse took Kylie to the nursery for me to get a good sleep. That's when I really missed her in the morning. When Kylie came back I cried with happiness when I held her. I could feel the love for Kylie, it was lovely. I feel guilty even now and she is nearly six years. Then I got my son two and a half years later. It was great. I wouldn't part with my family now, I love them all. When you see them in your stomach on the scanning screen it's great. But now they give you a photo of your unborn baby at five months. When I used to go for my antenatal care I had to have blood tests for Down's syndrome. They said they would let me know in a few weeks. But I was eight months before I had to ask the doctor what has happened to my result. He turned to say if it was a Down's syndrome baby they would have written to you early on. But I went through those weeks very scared, I thought they would have put my mind at rest.

42

'If you have an understanding manager you are OK'

I have two young daughters – the eldest is seven and the youngest is eighteen months. Our financial situation being what I expect 90 per cent of the population's is – a struggle at times – I had to go back to work after my eldest was born. I went back to work when she was five months old and I went back full-time. However, I used to get quite jealous of the childminder as my daughter was with her from 7.30 in the morning until 6 at night five days a week and I just felt I was no longer a 'proper' mother. I tolerated this for a year and I promised myself that by the time Lara (my daughter) was a year old I would be working part-time. Fortunately, the company I was working for then was run by a woman who had been through all the joys of being a working mother herself and was extremely fair and just towards any working mother who wanted to change her hours, etc. I had no problem in changing my hours – they were changed to three days a week, Tuesday, Wednesday and Thursday 8–4.30, which meant I had a long weekend with Lara every week. The drop in money was not as bad as I thought as I was saving on child-caring fees and the tax and National Insurance wasn't so high, so we were still able to just manage on my money. However, the drop in salary could not be matched by my feeling of happiness that I could now spend more time with Lara. It also led to a far less stressful home life, not having to get up at 5.45 every morning to leave the house for 7.30. It made a huge difference.

Now I come to the second phase of our family life!! I fell

pregnant with my second daughter when the company I worked for was amalgamated with another company – run by men – no woman held a major management position. I still had the usual maternity rights which I had no problems at all with. I came back to work when Rosie was six months old. Prior to falling pregnant, I had been asked to change my days to Monday, Tuesday and Wednesday, as my job had changed and I was now part of a job-share situation, and they felt they couldn't ask someone to work Monday, Wednesday and Friday – the crossover day being a Wednesday. However, I respected this and it is still working out OK. BUT the major difference is, I have been questioned on quite a few occasions about my hours (8–4.30), how did I manage to do this when the rest of the company work 9–5? I have been continually watched by directors (men) who check I am in and working at 8. There have been two occasions when I have been on the phone at about 8.20 in the morning (the caller called me) and a director has wanted to know why was I making phone calls and not working for the past 20 minutes (he starts at 8.15 and assumed wrongly on these occasions that I had been on the phone for 20 minutes). I have also learnt that all the other women who have been on maternity leave and come back to work since we have amalgamated with this male-dominated company have not had any cooperation with reduction in hours, etc. I am the last one that managed to get three days a week. The others have been told to work from 9–3.30 five days and that is as far as they will bend.

What upsets all the working mothers in our company is we are supposed to be recognized as an equal-opportunities company. Our head office in Glasgow apparently has excellent working terms and conditions for working parents and we are supposed to adopt this at a local level. However, this will not happen all the time. We have three out of the four directors saying 'Married women should be at home looking after the house and family.' When I first heard this comment had been made to one of the other mums I was outraged. Flexible working hours have been asked for on numerous occasions and have never got a fair hearing as they feel the system will be abused. The hours are supposed to be 9–5 but most managers accept that their staff work until 6–7 at night as par for the course!! To leave at 3.30 or 4.30 caused many a stir amongst management – are you skiving? – that sort of comment. They forget that we get paid less for doing less hours. I hate to say this but if we had a woman as a director or chief executive I am sure we would get a fair hearing, but whilst we have men running the company with Victorian attitudes we will get nowhere. If any of the women I work with have tried to take something further, they have been told 'If you don't like it . . .'

Another example has been recently when my eldest daughter was quite poorly for the first time in her life and I felt I couldn't send her to the childminder (remember this is the first time it had happened) and I had to ask for time off. In our personnel policy, it says that if there is no one else to look after a sick relative or the relative is too ill to leave, to take 'special leave'. I was told to take a day's holiday. The 'special leave' policy is left to management discretion – if you have an understanding manager you are OK, if you have a power-hungry man for a manager you don't stand a chance. I was more annoyed than anything else by the total lack of understanding and sympathy and the fact that it was the first time it had happened. Two weeks after this, my husband was taken into hospital and because of the treatment I had received with Lara I felt sure I was in for much of the same. However, they were far more understanding on this occasion, probably because my husband was in hospital.

Life is very difficult as a working mum. I am up and about from 5.45 in the morning and I don't stop until 8 at night when the children are in bed. I am just so glad it is for just three days a week. If it was five days a week, I think I would have cracked under the strain long ago. Plus knowing that the directors do not approve of the hours I work does not alleviate the pressure at all and I feel sure it is because I am a working mother. There is a very strong feeling of one rule for one and another for someone else. We do not have a car, so rely totally on public transport which is fortunately very good in our area. I am never late in the morning.

Other people roll into the office well after 9 some mornings and say it is because the children held them up. They do it continually and nothing is ever said to them. If I so much as answer a phone call before 9 a.m. I am clamped on straight away. I know that it isn't only me that gets treated like this. Most of the other working mothers do too, but for different things. The people that roll in late are usually the men and they get away with it! So, unfortunately, where I work there is no justice at all for working mothers and if we want to keep our jobs we just have to put up with it.

As far as child care is concerned, I pay £180 per month for my two children which is very reasonable. However, it is almost half my salary, but we need the other half to pay for groceries and clothes. We have an excellent registered childminder but help towards childminding fees would be extremely welcome. It would lift the pressure somewhat if the government increased Child Benefit to cover child care. I have to have a childminder and cannot rely on relations as they all live over 300 miles away. My mother-in-law cannot help out as her husband is an invalid, so we do not get out much because most of our friends also have children who would need looking after if we wanted a babysitter. They are also single parents so we could not even form a babysitting circle!

I truly wish I did not have to go out to work because I dearly love my two girls and there is nothing I would like better than to be with them. I always said what was the point in having children if you couldn't be with them? But because the cost of living these days is so high and we are not entitled to any help as we are just above the Family Credit line, I have to work and I work in a place made up mainly of men who have enough money for their wives to stay at home and look after the family. I hate this letter for sounding so despondent and negative but I feel that unless someone can change the attitude of men and single women in our company we will always hit the same problems. On a personal front, I have an extremely happy home life, my children are, so I am told, very well-balanced, happy-go-lucky little girls, so I don't think we have gone far wrong, do you?

'We cut down on fruit, meat'

Following the birth of my baby I found it very difficult to cope financially, and this led me to be very depressed. I already had one child of two and a half and my husband was earning £250 per week. Each month, we had to pay £420 out in insurance and mortgage, so we only had a few pounds to buy everything else – £30 a month goes on my eldest son's playgroup. We cut down on fruit, meat and ate as cheaply as possible. I was contributing to a private pension and life insurance fund but this had to stop as did the £5 per week I was saving for my older son. We do not go out socially and the children's clothes are given to them by relatives. The Child Benefit is spent towards shoes, but in no way is it sufficient to clothe them. The children do not have any treats provided by us. We only buy essential clothes for ourselves.

I was under a great deal of financial pressure to return to work full-time so I could provide adequately for them. My husband felt upset by this because he hoped to have been able to provide enough so I could work part-time. So he felt inadequate.

I get up at 4.45 a.m. to start work at 6 a.m. until 2.30 p.m. These hours fit in with baby-care arrangements and allow me time to be with the children in the afternoon. This also reduces the childminding cost which is £250 per month. It is a very difficult time – my wages go and yet there is the extra cost of nappies, baby food and milk.

'In the hostel . . . there was a great bond between us'

I am a 28-year-old part-time worker/mum and thought you might like to hear my point of view as I have seen life from both sides of the fence. When I had my daughter in 1992 I was in a stable relationship (not married) and had a good clerical job, a new car and we owned our own house. However, my partner and I split up when Emily was one year old and we went to live in a mother-and-baby hostel near my parents. Contrary to public opinion, including my own, I thoroughly enjoyed the six months in the hostel and though the women and often children had been through bad experiences, there was a great bond between us all.

During this time I met the man who became my husband and Emily's new dad. We married in April and that same week I began my job as a doctor's receptionist. I did twelve hours per week at £3.15 per hour. Believe me, a doctor's receptionist does a lot more than answer the phone, etc. I was expected to do all sorts of medical things, for example, give test results and sort out vaccinations, etc. Eventually, I decided that getting Emily to the childminder by 8 a.m. and being on tenterhooks all day wasn't worth that kind of money, so I resigned. Luckily, I got another job straight away in an office just five minutes away from home which made things much easier. This was sixteen hours a week and my lady boss has three young children herself, so she knows the pressures of illness or lack of a sitter and we reached a casual agreement straight away. I was also paid £3.50 an hour which is the most you can get to avoid tax and NI [National Insurance] payments. I'm still there now and love every minute of it.

Now, however, there's another complication. I'm expecting another baby in August and therefore I will have to give up my job as there is no way I can afford child care for two children. My husband is on a decent salary and we haven't got hefty bills or a large mortgage. We have about £300 of goods on HP [hire purchase]. Even saying all this we still only just manage on his wages, and mine buys all the little extras. We don't go out and don't smoke or rent videos, etc. I'd like to know how this can happen in today's society. The government tells us we should take more responsibility for our children so that they don't all turn into drug addicts or vandals. Yet they don't give married mothers any support whatsoever. When I was a single parent I was offered every benefit available – free college places with a crèche, child-care allowance if I went back to work, etc. To be honest I was much better off financially when I was single than I am now. It seems these days you are penalized for giving your child a stable, loving and, dare I say it, two-parent environment.

45

'£1 over the Income Support limit'

My husband left me and my two children six years ago. Before he left we had a lovely house, a nice car and I had a part-time job, which I loved, for a social research institute in London. After he left my life had to change dramatically. I desperately tried to continue working but without a car this proved impossible. Eventually, I reluctantly went on Income Support. I had to sell the house and buy a smaller one. When the Child Support Agency first assessed my husband, the amount he had to pay took me £1 over the Income Support limit. I then had to find a job which gave me enough hours in order to claim Family Credit. It also had to be school hours only and somewhere I could take the children in school holidays. I have 8 O levels and 3 A levels and found that the only job I was able to do was cleaning people's houses. I ended up having to take four jobs to make up the sixteen hours. That was two years ago. I'm still cleaning now and I will continue to do so until the children are old enough to be left. I've noticed as I've applied for cleaning jobs how there are more and more educated women applying for those same jobs. It's one of the few jobs that will fit in with looking after school-age children.

My confidence and self-esteem are so low now that I can imagine it's going to be really difficult to get a full-time job – after all, who is going to employ someone who has been a cleaner for years? It's also hard on the children when their standard of living has to change. They also find it embarrassing to have to admit that their mum's a cleaner. It seems to me that more and more women who find themselves as single parents have to resort to lower-paid work simply to make ends meet, whereas the fathers who leave can stay in their jobs.

46

'When I found out I was pregnant . . . I was only thirteen'

When I found out I was pregnant with my first child I was only thirteen. I moved into my mother's big bedroom. My mum and dad moved into the little back bedroom, two brothers in another bedroom and my other two brothers in the attic. While I was pregnant, I couldn't get help from anywhere and because my dad worked that made it worse. If my dad was unemployed I would have been able to get help. When my first child Andrew was born I was in the hospital six days. I came home and I was home about an hour and a half, and a knock came on the door. It was a social worker. He came in and he asked me if I needed help with the baby when it was born and I was sitting on the settee feeding him. He saw I was feeding the baby and went. I never saw him again.

The only income I had coming in was the Child Benefit. So in my bedroom at that time was my bed, Andrew's cot, my wardrobe and Andrew's cupboards. So my bedroom was full. Then a year and a half later I found out I was pregnant again, at that time I was fourteen. Still couldn't get any help. When my second child was born I was fifteen. The same people were living in the house so I had to squeeze everything into my room, so in my room now was my bed, my eldest child's bed, my baby's cot and all our wardrobes. When I was fifteen and a half I went to the council to see if I could have my own place. They told me to fill in a housing form, send it back and when I was sixteen they would consider me for a house of my own. When I became sixteen I went up to the council and they told me I couldn't have a house until I was eighteen. They said somebody should have contacted me to tell me. So my boyfriend had to fill in a housing form. We made an appointment to see somebody to get a house of our own. They told us to look at some empty houses and go back. We saw some houses, we went back and told the council that we would take a house. So we had the keys in November. But due to repairs we couldn't move in until February. They told me I would be classed as a lodger until I was eighteen. My name wouldn't be able to go on the rent book until I was eighteen.

47

'A big family event'

As a mother of two children under three and a half I am writing to give you a Sikh perspective of motherhood in this country. Having a baby in the Asian community is a big family event. The extended family comes forth in support of the mother and baby. In both instances, when I had my children, my mother-in-law came (from Wolverhampton) to look after both the baby and me. She stayed for 40 days after the delivery. Traditionally, the pregnant woman goes to her mother's house to be cared for after the delivery, but in case she is not available then the mother-in-law steps in. During the 40 days, the mother and baby are taken to the Gurudwara [Sikh temple] and prayers are said for the baby's long life. The Guru Granth Sahib [Sikh's holy book] is opened randomly by the priest. The first letter of the first word on this randomly opened page is the chosen letter for naming the baby. In my case this started a six-week period of extensive consultation and debate on what to name the baby. During this time my children were known only as 'Baby M' and 'Baby A'. I wanted their names to mean something instead of just anything that sounded good. So Baby M was named Mehr meaning 'a blessing' and Baby A was named Achint meaning 'one who has no worries'.

I was not allowed to do any housework or cook during the 40-day period. Both baby and I were given a massage daily before our baths. This was wonderful and relieved much of the pain in my legs which was much in evidence when I breast-fed. I breast-fed Mehr for sixteen months as he would not take the bottle, and

Achint for ten months. I probably would have breast-fed her for longer except that she started teething at three and a half months and breast-feeding became quite uncomfortable with her constantly biting me and making me sore!

I was given lots of different foods to eat during the 40-day period. This was so that the baby could get used to all the variety of foods the mother was likely to eat. Spices, etc., were kept to the minimum while I was breast-feeding. I was given a sweet dish made of butter, plain flour, ginger and nuts ground together. This is a nourishing dish containing many vitamins and minerals and is considered to be an essential part of the diet of a new mother, especially one that is breast-feeding. It is also served to all those who come to see the baby. I was not allowed to drink plain water or fizzy drinks. Water to which fennel and other herbs were added was boiled, strained and cooled, and only then given to me to drink. This was so that the baby did not get wind.

I had to return to work or I would lose my job and then we couldn't have managed. Now that I am back at work part-time, my parents look after my children. I don't have to do anything except to drop the children at my parents in the morning and from then on they feed them, bathe them and play with them. When I return from work my mother has my evening meal ready because she feels that I need to spend time with my children and not have the bother of cooking. She feels that since she is going to be cooking anyway she just has to increase the amount she cooks and there is not much extra effort involved for her, whereas it would take up a lot of my time. Finally, I cannot imagine how working mothers cope without any family support – I would have found it impossible to bring up my children without all this unconditional help from my parents and in-laws. I have been extremely lucky in having this support and wish all mothers could have it as well.

48

'When will I get back to work?'

I am no longer a working mum because I found it too difficult to afford and find suitable, trustworthy child-care arrangements. My husband and I have both worked since leaving school, we have three children and are now really struggling to make ends meet. My husband works shifts with no identifiable pattern, this has made it increasingly difficult for me to go to work. I only worked evenings from 4.45–9.15 p.m. but the strain of wondering whether my babysitter would be available, having to have time off if she wasn't available, took its toll and I had to leave work. I couldn't find a registered childminder because they were charging more than I earned. I worked for a large biscuit manufacturers in Manchester who, although they employ mostly women, will not create a crèche in the workplace, because of the money involved.

My husband earns £12,000 per annum before tax, a lot you might think but we have to run a house, run a car (that my husband needs for work) and three children on that. We are just above the maximum for getting help with benefits; therefore we have to pay full Council Tax, pay for school dinners, prescriptions, eye tests and dental treatment. It makes me very angry to see people who through fault of their own have no job or any intention of getting one living the life of Reilly. Paying no rent, no Council Tax, free milk, free school meals, uniform grants, free prescriptions, dental treatment and eye tests. We have paid tax and National Insurance for fifteen years (apart from when on maternity leave) and basically have ended up with nothing. I can't ask my mum to look after the children as she works full-time and has angina. When will I get back to work? Who knows? Even when all three children are at school I would have to earn a dynamic wage to pay for child care, especially in the school holidays.

49

'We had to bring our own sheets and blankets'

At the births of my two children, my son in December 1990 and my daughter in May 1993, I was a single parent receiving Income Support. My partner worked in London, I live in Belfast and we only see each other maybe five times in a year. At the birth of my son I was very surprised that we had to bring our own sheets and blankets for the baby's cot, and as my son was born four weeks premature I had nothing ready for him. My mother had to buy the sheets for me. The choice would have been to let the newborn baby sleep on threadbare sheets and blankets that the hospital supplied. At the birth of my daughter nothing had changed.

50

'He was going to the jewellers
to get me a gold band'

Having attended all my parentcraft classes like a good girl, it was a shock when I went into labour. The pain was incredible, it lasted for 36 hours. In that period various nurses and midwives came, made placating noises, took blood pressures, gave me epidural, etc., but nobody allowed me to move from the bed. It took a lot of beseeching and talking on my part to get a doctor in to explain to me why it was taking so long. Maybe it was my persistence (troublemaker from their point of view) but eventually they decided that everything was not quite right. Blood samples from the foetus were taken at regular intervals, each reading indicated that the oxygen level was falling. After the third reading, a flurry of activities happened. I was made ready for an emergency Caesarean operation because the baby was in danger. I don't remember much about what happened for 24 hours after the operation. I was too far gone and drugged up. Eventually I surfaced. I remember my husband saying that we had a baby boy and that he was going to the jewellers to get me a gold band ring for my third finger of the left hand because he objected to the fact that the staff assumed I was an unmarried mother since I was not wearing one. Why was I not wearing one? Because it is not necessary in the Asian culture – there is no one ring to symbolize the marriage pact, we receive many jewellery pieces which are worn and taken off depending on the circumstances.

On the third day I was given a bed bath after I had breast-fed the baby for the first time. The staff helped me to put on the bra saying 'Let's shove 'em in then.' That really gave my ego a boost! Soon after I developed a temperature, due to an infection. I was washed down with a cold cloth and the fan was turned on full blast to bring the temperature down. The shock on my mother's face when she came to visit was explosive. Back home, the new mother is shielded from chills and winds of any kind for at least ten days if not 40. The sight of seeing me naked with the fan full blast was not conducive to her way at all. Now in cold weather I feel the chill on my legs more than any other part of my body. She is convinced it is because of the fan which has chilled my bones for life.

'My mother was great'

I am a single mother bringing up my baby on my own. My family are very supportive towards me and without them, I do not know how I would get by. I spent some time in London where I discovered that first-time mothers do not get enough help with bringing up their children. They are left to their own devices, which I think is wrong, because I was very scared and nervous towards my baby.

My mother was great. She gave me all the guidance I needed. Single mothers do not get enough money to live on. Children need a lot of things at all times and I found it difficult to live on the money I got. By the time I got most things for my child there was not much left to feed myself. We should also get more help with paying bills. It is very worrying when you have no money and no one to turn to and children's clothes, nappies and food are all very expensive. I get most of my clothes given to me because I could not afford to buy them. I also find that single mothers are looked down on too much, but I think they should be given more credit. Due to domestic violence I am forced to bring my child up on my own, but I do it the best I can. Love is stronger than any need.

'All the pleasure in the world'

I am 23 years old, and my baby is 26 days old. This is my first child. I am working full-time in a garment factory as a sewing machinist. My partner is also working full-time. He is divorced and has three children from his first marriage. I am one of the fortunate ones who had nearly everything I needed before, during and after the pregnancy. This may be because both my husband and I work very, very hard to earn money and also spend it more wisely. I was eating reasonably good healthy food but could have done better. I had a good healthy baby girl and I thank Almighty Allah for this, without whose help this could not have been possible.

With my experience I can say that the Child Support Agency's rules need to be reviewed again as they put more emphasis on the children from the marriage, who in most of the cases are not living with their fathers and yet get more money. The newly born baby gets less yet baby gives all the joy, happiness, gives will to live and all the pleasure in the world.

Hospital facilities before and during the pregnancy are very good but they should keep mother and baby at least seven days in hospital after the birth, which would give much needed rest to mother. Also paternity leave should be increased to at least ten working days.

'I lost my flat,
car and job'

I left school at fifteen years old to support my family as my step-father passed away, leaving mum with seven children, myself being the eldest. My first son was born when I was nineteen years old and my second when I was 23 years. I continually worked full-time within weeks of both their births. During the recession I lost my flat, car and job, but had some money so did not sign on. During the past four years I have had to sign on as unemployed.

I did a college course in computer applications to enable me to return to secretarial work as one has to be computer literate these days. Even though I have twelve years of secretarial experience, no one will employ you if you cannot work a computer. This course, which is available under the government's Training for Work scheme, is a farce, to say the least. Most of the time I had to share a computer because of the overcrowding in class. There were, some days, approximately 50 students to one tutor. During my attendance at computer college I was twice taken off an exam paper to look after their reception because they had staff shortages. I complained but was wasting my breath. Apparently when one commences a Training for Work scheme you sign a declaration stating that you are at the college's disposal. I tried to get the Job Centre to transfer me, but because of the government's shut-downs on local colleges the nearest college was Streatham. The only alternative and the course I intend to take is for me to pay for my own seat.

During this time I was ill and being treated by my GP for IBS [irritable bowel syndrome] which is a nervous complaint. It was only five months later, when I was referred to a gynaecology consultant for a suspected ovarian cyst, that I had a scan and was informed that I was twenty weeks pregnant. The distress is unimaginable because I was taking so many different pills that I could not imagine the baby not being affected. However, after numerous tests, the time was slipping by and when the results were made available, it was too late for a termination, although the hospital was extremely reluctant to offer this. I had to raise the subject myself and was side-stepped around this possibility. I am assured that my baby is normal and have been put under the clinic at the hospital to deal with my IBS. However, I have recently had a biopsy and they have discovered that I now have colitis – inflammation of the bowel and intestine – so I am on more drugs to control this.

I have an off-and-on relationship with my boyfriend and we do not need this added pressure but as this baby has survived the impossible, he deserves a fair chance in life. I am going to continue my studies after my baby is born and support us. The baby's father is also willing to support us when he is quite sure that the baby is OK and has not been affected by all the medication I have been on. All I want at the moment is to give my baby a start in life but this is not easy. I applied for a budget loan from the DSS [Department of Social Security] to buy the main essentials for him, such as a cot, mattress, blankets, sheets, bottles, sterilizer, babygrows, etc. These items have become so expensive since I last bought them seventeen years ago. I rang to see how my application was coming along, only to be told the government have decided no payments are to be made against maternity items. What the hell is this and why? I am going to an interview today because I appealed against this idiotic decision, and they are apparently going to give me a reason for this decision – I can't wait to hear this!!

I am 40 years of age with two grown-up children. I have worked full-time since I was fifteen and just happen to have had a rough time over the last four years since my crash, after the recession. I have always paid my way and even paid single tax as a married woman. Do the government think they can treat people this way?

54

'Let down by the system'

My story is a good illustration of how women can still be let down by the system in this country, despite supposed advances through the century. In particular, it concerns shortcomings in the Legal Aid system, in the newly set up Child Support Agency (CSA), and recent legislation which was apparently designed to help women but has in fact proved easy to circumvent. This is the Trade Union Reform and Employment Rights Act (TURERA) which came into force in 1992. I believe their shortcomings arise from a lack of flexibility – they were designed to safeguard women in one specific situation alone. For example, the legal process in making a financial settlement after divorce, when there is disagreement, is tortuously slow and difficult (it has so far taken me three years, and the minimum is about six months). This protects women who remain in the former matrimonial home with their children. But I fled with my sons and my first husband still lives in the house, and so he is protected while we had to struggle to find a home. There should be a 'quickie' process which ensures that the parent with custody either lives in the family home or can control the timing of its sale, with immediate effect after custody is established.

But I am jumping the gun. I married at 28 in 1987 and immediately conceived a boy, born early at 36 weeks. The following year I had a second son, born three weeks late. I was divorced within six years, because of my then husband's verbal and physical abuse of me. A year later I remarried, and with my new husband had a third son, induced two weeks post-term in November 1994.

My first husband earned more than the Prime Minister, around £50,000 a year, but being self-employed was able to divert most of his income away from the household. He tended to feed it into business ventures which were clearly doomed from the start. Our large four-bed detached was largely funded from my parents' life savings. When we divorced, I had to flee the house or risk being murdered (I still do not doubt this) and my ex-husband is now virtually a sitting tenant so that all that money is lost. Because I am on Legal Aid, I cannot take the action I would wish, the action that is needed, to recover my money. For the last three years, my ex has cleverly agreed to a sale in principle. My solicitor advises me that this is sufficient indication of willingness to sell for the Legal Aid to refuse me permission for the expensive item of court action. Yet the alternative of numerous letters of negotiation has proved more costly. Moreover, my ex is not paying the mortgage and since I am joint owner, this debt is accruing under my name as well as his. In the meantime, he stonewalls by lying that 'I'll put it on the market in six months when I've saved a bit' or similar. So I have had to watch helplessly as he stays put. He refuses to maintain the house, but has changed the locks so that I cannot gain entry. Of course, I could not have afforded a divorce without Legal Aid, but it is too functionally dependent on solicitors who would like to protect their income from your case (and yes, even maximize it). This means avoiding expensive single items which might induce the Legal Aid team to inspect the cost of a case and rap the solicitor's knuckles for unnecessary overspending. Lots of cheap items can be more easily blamed on the client! Perhaps an independent assessment board could be set up to evaluate the need for court action.

My financial situation is much worse than ever before. My second husband earns less than I do when I work, which is not saying much. But we are a very happy family. We have just had our first child, half-brother to my other children. His birth unfortunately cost me my much-loved job. The letter of notice was inconceivable to me, because TURERA became effective just in time for my dismissal to be unlawful. TURERA says that a pregnant woman cannot lose her job, no matter how short her working hours. It is also embodied in this law that a woman now has the right to return to her own job after maternity leave, and not simply a similar job as before. She can still be made redundant if she is truly so (and not as a result of her pregnancy) but in this case she must be given first choice of an alternative job. Minimum maternity-leave entitlements have also been established for all women, regardless of length of service. And so when I received notice the day my baby was due, I knew that I should appeal. I worked at a hospital and was certain I had been seen as a soft target because of my (statutory) maternity leave; the hospital had merged with another and needed to show good end-of-year figures. The hospital quickly admitted that they had acted unlawfully, but all they had to do to make things legal was to temporarily reinstate me after my statutory maternity leave was officially over, and then reissue the notice! So we are now scraping an existence at the very time that we actually need more money, not less; it is not exactly easy to go to job interviews with a very tiny, new-born baby. I am sad that with any new job I will have to leave my baby locally and so cease breast-feeding earlier than I had wanted. I breast-fed the first two boys until they were thirteen months old, and, if I had continued to work at the hospital, could have fed my third son easily, at the crèche at the hospital.

Unfortunately, and ironically given its brief when it was set up, the new Child Support Agency has ensured that we get no help from my ex-husband. He is self-employed and has three companies so that his large salary can be hidden by devious accounting. Under the old child-maintenance system, I could go to court and ask for information about his companies and bank accounts. Now I have to rely on the CSA, which has more limited powers than the courts. My ex has got away with having to pay the minimum assessment of £2.20 per week simply by refusing to tell the CSA what he earns. Yet I am redundant and earn nothing, while he earns around £50,000 a year.

But my tale is not all woe and gloom. My second husband, who is five years younger than me, is a wonderful man who has taken on the dreadful responsibilities of step-parenting while the children's natural father abandons their welfare, liaising with him to protect me, and losing all his annual leave on court attendances and visits to Social Services for interim reports between court appearances. I dread to think how other women cope, especially those who do not find new partners, when there is so little professional support. I am glad to say that my second husband is a New Man. Nineties Man. He occupies himself with the baby as much as I do, and we are now considering swapping roles since I can command a better salary than him. I cannot say I shall like to be away from my baby at all, but the arrangement will be for his good.

55

'I would always choose debt rather than do without'

I have been a single parent for sixteen years. Until six years ago I was in receipt of full Income Support. Considering I raised my children with absolutely no financial help from my ex-husband (an alcoholic who claimed that his psychological problems prevented him from working), the money I received from the DSS [Department of Social Security] was barely adequate. I had enough for food and bills but not for clothes (for them or me), newspapers, toys, treats, bus fares (we lived on the outskirts of our town). I always had a part-time job on the go, but this never paid enough. My major problem was that the more money I could get my hands on, the greater my desire for an even higher standard of living. I could never accept that this was my situation and I should get on with it. Consequently, I find myself now in a relatively well-paid job and mammoth debts rooted in those early days when I refused not to take my children on holiday, or buy them new bikes because their friends had them. I was grateful to Access for giving me a credit card, but alarmed by the ease with which a person, a sole parent on full Income Support, could acquire one.

I never found bringing up, actually parenting, my children a difficult job. In fact, I thought (and still think) they're wonderful. Combining motherhood and a part-time job was hard, but I never found it a grind. My major problem was always lack of money, and I would always choose debt rather than do without, but having said that, I always worked, sometimes for a pittance and sometimes a lot more than I was entitled to earn on Income Support. I am absolutely certain that Income Support does not give a sole parent enough to have an acceptable standard of living. But my ex-husband should take responsibility for never even giving his children their pocket-money, let alone hardly ever remembering Christmas and birthdays.

56

'A mum and overworked and underpaid teacher'

I am a 36-year-old mother of two children – Tom, aged sixteen months, and Sarah, aged three, are a dream. My husband Tim and I tried for almost three years to have a child and eventually, after many tests and a laparoscopy, I fell pregnant. Sarah was born in July 1992 and I was unsure whether I wanted to return to my teaching job in the local comprehensive. When the time came for the decision to be made I felt quite sure I wanted to return as long as I could work part-time. This was discussed and agreed. I returned to work when Sarah was seven months old, happy in the thought that with my salary we would be able to provide that much more for Sarah, and I also felt I would be that much fresher to cope with the demands of a toddler than I might have been if I had been at home all the time. I would not have returned to work if I had to go full-time as I had been previously, although I'm not sure we could have managed financially. However, I did feel that I had not got the patience and maybe not the inclination to stay at home to 'mother' all the time. I needed more! Perhaps if I had had children in my twenties it would have been different, but being an older mum, used to her independence, I would have found it very difficult.

Finding a suitable childminder was a nightmare, although in the end we were very lucky. I told myself many times that – yes, someone else could look after my child just as well as I could and in reality probably even better. It was sometimes hard to juggle the job with a small child. The general population seem to think teachers have it easy, finishing 'in the middle of the afternoon' and having thirteen weeks' holiday a year. Sure it's a bonus, but like most teachers I found myself working late into the evening when Sarah was in bed – marking, planning for the next day or week, setting exams, writing records of achievement and general administration.

Getting up early with a small child is never easy, never mind getting to work on time, and while Sarah has always been a good sleeper, there have been nights when our sleep was disturbed some-times for a couple of hours, resulting in parents who go to work looking and feeling less than perfect. The strains of managing despite a supportive husband sometimes showed and life was made no easier with the occasional comment from someone who made it clear they thought I should be at home caring for my child 100 per cent of the time. I had to remind myself on more than one occasion that I was indeed supporting my child by going out to work.

Certainly people expect a lot from teachers and it is necessary to give 100 per cent commitment, but some staff and parents need to remember that most teachers do have a life out of school. For others, maybe they need reminding that times have changed since they had their children. A colleague of mine related a tale recently from when she returned to work having had her second child. Every lunch-time Julie went home to breast-feed Thomas and every afternoon when she returned to school, the head teacher (a man) was standing at the door of her room to check on her timekeeping. When on the third day after returning from maternity leave Julie was a couple of minutes late, she received an official letter from the head with a warning.

Certain staff have been known to make a quip in the staffroom about mothers returning to work for pin money – they seem to think it is funny! All these people make me feel selfish and inad-equate, they all make me feel like I am doing it rightly or wrongly for the money and they all make me feel guilty. My husband says I shouldn't feel guilty and so do my friends who work, but I still sometimes am made to feel like a bad mother. It's difficult not to.

After fourteen months I left the school for my second pregnancy and Tom was born May 1994. I kept my part-time job open and decided to go back when he was seven months old. When I had been back a few weeks, I really didn't want to be there. The job was fine despite lots of work outside school hours, but for some reason I found it more difficult leaving my son than I ever did leaving Sarah the first time round. I wanted to be at home with my children. Perhaps it was because this time I knew I wouldn't have any more babies and I didn't want to miss a minute of Tom's early development. Now, nine months later, I'm back after the summer vacation feeling as if I've never been away. It is so easy to slip back into the routine despite all the changes in the education system (just another reason for wanting to stay in my job rather than leaving for a few years). Sarah is happy at nursery. Tom is happy at the childminder's. I remember a friend advising me when I returned to work the first time that I would worry if Sarah did not want to go to the childminder, but I would be just as upset if she didn't want to come home with me when I picked her up. Sarah has only feigned this act a few times but it has nevertheless reassured me of her happiness while she is away from me.

I still have some concerns, like worrying about falling asleep in a meeting when I've been awake six times in the night, or worrying about asking other colleagues to cover for me when one or both of the children are ill. However, the one thing that must pull at every working mother's heart-strings, as it did at mine, is the bewildered little face when you leave your pride and joy at the childminder's for the first time.

A mum and overworked and underpaid teacher.

'It has all been worth it'

At eighteen I fell pregnant by accident. I told my parents who said they would support me. My partner said he would stand by me but four months into my pregnancy he left me. My pregnancy had no complications. I was living in a one-bedroomed flat at the time and receiving £28 a week Income Support. I received a £100 Maternity Payment. My father helped financially. Without that help, I know I could not have managed. In September 1994 I gave birth to my son, Jed. My family were very supportive. I have been very lucky. In August last year I decided to work part-time. The money was the main reason but I was determined not to be an unemployed single mother for ever. Luckily, between my mother and best friend, my child-care costs are very low. I am on Family Credit and receive some money from Jed's dad.

Although I am only slightly better off, working has other benefits. Jed and I have a break from each other. We seem now to appreciate each other more. I still find myself counting every penny but I knew it would not be easy. Sometimes I wonder why I do it, but then I stand back and look at my boy and I know it has all been worth it. Who knows, one day I may win the lottery and I won't have to count the pennies any more!

'Sanitary protection can be quite difficult financially'

My daughter, Anna, is twenty months old. We have been on our own since May 1994 and living in shared temporary accommodation, whilst waiting to be housed permanently through the local council. The income I receive each week is £76.50. Whilst I think I budget quite well, mostly relying on monthly payments to club books, a store card for my daughter's shoes and monthly payments to people such as TV licensing, every pound is accounted for, which means simple things like haircuts and sanitary protection can be quite difficult financially. It usually results in cutting down on food for myself that week. However, I do try to make sure my daughter eats as healthily as she will allow!

Whilst living on benefits I have given a lot of thought about returning to work, though unfortunately after taking into account outgoings such as bus fares and childminders, there is no incentive to do so. Because of this and the time I have to myself each evening, I have decided to study an Open Learning course in child psychology resulting in a GCSE exam. This I hope will help me in the future. Once Anna starts school full-time, I intend to begin a career in nursery-school teaching/helping, which will fit in well with Anna's school holidays. There is three years between now and Anna starting school, which I have planned to fill doing various courses at home with regard to my career change (I was a baker before Anna's birth). This is probably the only benefit in receiving Income Support – the courses are usually free. I have recently been to a solicitor to make a will. Being single I want to be certain of

Anna's future upbringing. This is also free if receiving benefits, something which I believe should be made far more public.

I strongly believe more should be done as regards the absent parent. Personally speaking I have received nothing from Anna's father since the day I left. He refuses to pay maintenance, even though the Child Support Agency are involved. His main criticism being why should he support me as well as Anna? I think it's extremely important to look ahead and not dwell on the present day, there are a few advantages to receiving benefits as I have already stated. That's not to say I haven't had my share of tears, bitterness, sleepless nights and regret, that took many months to come to terms with before I felt ready to begin life again. And now, although times are hard financially, at least I have a positive feeling inside myself knowing it won't last for ever. I know now I made the right decision to leave my partner, and now look forward to a much happier future for myself and Anna.

59

'A hole in the net of cover'

I have been a single mum for thirteen years now. My ex-husband left me with our three children aged eleven years, six years and 23 months on Christmas Day 1981. He had been seeing another woman and despite a valiant try the marriage broke up. I had some food in the house and £10 in money when he went. I had moved to the Midlands in the middle of November and was not really even settled in properly. I knew no one, was not on the telephone, no transport. My mother and father were living in South Wales, my sister in Yorkshire, so I had no one at all.

My first problem was to get help from the DSS [Department of Social Security]. I was in a very distressed state and can't remember much about that interview. My mother and father had travelled up 200 miles to help and my mother sorted that first interview for me. They could only stay a few days and then I was on my own again. My second problem was getting the two older children back to school. I told both schools the facts and would implore parents to do the same. Children can be watched for signs of trouble such as aggression, falling standards and emotional outbursts. School trips and things like PE kits etc. were a big problem, as they always need those things when the big bills come in. Schools give little time usually for you to plan for an outing. Now these trips can be free, how long for who knows. Keeping in line with educational trends such as being told to watch videos and listen to tapes can be a problem as Income Support doesn't really run to these expenses.

The eldest child, Martin, was ill during his fourth year in senior school. Because of this he had to retake the year. The result of this was that he was nineteen years old before he finished his A levels. With five months of the A level course to run, seven months before he would take up a university place, all money for him stopped. At the DSS I was told that this was a hole in the net of cover, nothing they could do about it, could he not leave and take his A levels at college or forget about them and get a job? I said 'No way, but how do I afford to keep him? Do I throw him out then you would have to do something?' The reply was 'Yes, but as you have said that, we would take that into consideration when dealing with the case.' I then went to a money advisory service at the local council. She wrote to several places and finally got two grants from an independent trust which almost covered the amount I would lose. He got his A levels and went to Birmingham University where in 1994 he got a B.Sc. Hons. degree. He now has a job as a department manager in a retail firm and lives away from home.

My eldest daughter is doing her A levels now and has five months to go. One of her subjects is drama. We have difficulty in affording trips to the theatre to see plays as transport and tickets are costly. She wants to go to university and take French and become a teacher. This is a four-year course. Viewing universities is difficult cost-wise again. She has managed a couple. I know she will do her best but I worry about how she will manage as grants are due to be cut by 10 per cent. Laura is a clever, lovely girl.

The result of Laura leaving home has another aspect. The money Emily, aged fourteen, and I receive will go down by nearly £40 to £60–70 including my Child Benefit. I know my rent and housing tax is free and I get prescriptions and dental care free and discount on water rates, but it is very little money to pay for food, clothing, household expenses, entertainment, insurance. I know that my mother on a pension gets almost as much to keep herself as I will get for the two of us. Allowances for a fourteen–fifteen-year-old come to £23.60. An eight-year-old in foster care gets £45–48 plus holiday pay and birthday allowances. To keep a child in care is in excess of £120 per week. So my child is worth so much less than them. She is a very good girl, never asks for things she knows I can't afford. I would like to work but am torn between leaving her alone during holidays, etc. I know she is the sort of child who misses me and needs me to be there when she comes home. I am also now out of touch with work. I can address this I know. I also suffer with arthritis in the hands, back and feet which at times flares into a debilitating condition. Heavy work is out, I did part-time in a café and I had to give it up in the end. Can I earn enough to make it worthwhile my going to work? I am 44 years old now. I feel I have failed to give my children the things that so many take for granted and fear Emily's life until she can work will be poorer than the others.

Yes, I have three bright, beautiful children, I have done all I can but because my husband deserted me and the children we are penalized and are branded by the media as the cause of the ills of society. Yes, I have been lucky, relatives have taken us on holiday, my sister lives by the sea and we have had breaks away. People have taken Emily away with them to keep their children company, she is a popular little girl. But it's hard to be unable to pay for things yourself. There is a very great amount of strain involved in looking after children and not having that special person to say it's alright, to be unable to share the wonderful things as well as the sad or painful things that happen. You always feel you are not in control of your life at all. I fear so much going under and getting into debt. After all these years, the big things like cooker, suite, bed, linen, washing machine are getting old. I can't replace them, can't afford to replace them. I am not looking forward to the future as it is so scary. Even now my self-esteem is still quite low. Managing on a low income and getting lower in ever-increasing ways takes everything out of you and in the end there is little left inside to fight on with.

I hope this is not too long to read, perhaps it puts a little of the way of life on Income Support long-term. I would not have kept a full-time job as illness has dogged us all through the year – asthma, glandular fever, all sorts – besides, children need someone to come home to.

60

'Hard work never killed anyone'

I found out that I was pregnant in July 1985. My boyfriend, Sam, and I had recently returned from an eight-month trip to South America – a 'year out' before the final year of our degree courses. It was a few days before my 21st birthday and I'd been putting it off for so long that I knew I had to be over two months gone already. I knew right then that I'd be having the baby, but I promised Sam and my mum that we'd consider everything thoroughly. After a week or so of soul-searching we could only agree that it would be difficult either way. Sam's main fear was that we wouldn't cope financially, that neither of us would successfully complete our final year if we had a small child to raise, mainly because the grant is so feeble these days. I proposed that we take turns to complete our courses, Sam first for obvious reasons, and that we would survive on benefit, as millions have to. But however confident I felt, it cannot be denied that the outlook was far from rosy.

When we got back to Brighton, where we're both based for college, we decided to keep the baby and went to the student-welfare office. Already things were stacked against us – Sam's grant would be deducted from our benefit, fair enough (so would his loan entitlement, whether or not he took one out), but what we could not understand was that £17 a week of his grant would be deducted again from any Housing Benefit we received, leaving us £17 short of the Income Support rate for a couple. To add insult to injury, when the baby was born even Child Benefit was deducted! I wish I could remember how it felt to be surprised that a benefit intended for 'everybody' has been taken from the poorest group in society!

I got some work temporarily in a delicatessen, an old Saturday job from the first and second years, while Sam dived head-first into house-hunting. What with chopping and changing our plans for house-sharing, we ended up going it alone and after six long weeks we found a lovely one-bedroom flat for £85 a week. Those six weeks were possibly the hardest. We were staying with different friends and Sam couldn't get work while he was house-hunting despite our still owing money from our return journey from South America. He also needed to start studying ready for the autumn and became increasingly frustrated, trekking all over the place to view properties and being constantly mucked around by landlords. To top it off we didn't have enough cash to secure a place anyway! During this period, Sam called the Benefit Agency several times, resulting in the spirit-crushing discovery that I am not entitled to Income Support or Housing Benefit, whether or not I am working and even though I am pregnant, because I am an 'intermitting student' (intending to return to college the following year). The telephonist who broke this to Sam was as horrified himself as we were, I believe. He felt that we'd have better luck when I was 29 weeks pregnant and would therefore no longer have to make myself available for work in order to claim. Sam wrote letters of outrage to the local MP and councillors, always receiving the same reply – 'The government makes the policies, we just implement them.' We even received one letter, from the Brighton and Hove Council Welfare Rights Service, to whom Sam's letter had been forwarded, saying that our position was 'even worse than you think'. It pointed out that I would not be eligible for any benefit until the baby was actually born, because students, intermitting or otherwise, can only claim when they are 'responsible for a child' who is 'normally living with you', which apparently cannot be said of a pregnant woman. Incidentally, we would still be eligible to pay 75 per cent of the full Council Tax rate (25 per cent is deducted as Sam is a student!) as the taxation department conveniently considers me not to be a student at all. Luckily I managed to secure my job, but the business then changed hands and both my hours and my hourly rate were cut, leaving me with £92.50 take-home pay for a 37-hour week which included two days working 9 a.m.–2 p.m. and 5 p.m.–9 p.m. With the flat being a half an hour's walk away this had me on my feet from 8.30 a.m. till 9.30 p.m., with two hours at home to eat lunch and 'crash out'. After our rent we had £7.50 a week more than Sam's maintenance grant between us.

We moved into the flat at the beginning of October, with Sam's parents lending us the £350 deposit (the initial layout on the flat was £718 – deposit plus a month's rent in advance). An entire term's grant is £659.75. At last we felt we were beginning to settle. Sam worked evenings in an office to pay off the overdraft, putting him behind in his studies. Eventually the long-awaited 29-week 'deadline' arrived and with bated breath I submitted a claim. Having the benefit of foresight I 'avoided' mentioning my status as an intermitting student. Fortunately the situation is fairly uncommon and this fact has so far eluded the powers that be. After the obligatory weeks in limbo we received notification, first of Income Support and finally of Housing and Council Tax Benefit – we were lucky. Paradoxically, we are now better off than most of our fellow students whose grant doesn't even stretch as far as their rent. While we recognize that our current income is as minimalist as it could be in relation to our outgoings, we certainly cannot complain. Many people don't have their families' support as we do and, moreover, we've had to face the prospect of being completely abandoned by the welfare state.

Now, with the baby due in three short weeks, I see not hardship before us but hard work and that never killed anyone! Time will tell whether we can both pass our courses with the baby growing up and whether Sam will be able to be a full-time parent whilst I am trying, or whether the benefit system will find new ways to let us down. We're hoping to have the baby at home and the policy here in Brighton seems to be 'Why not?' which is wonderful for us, this being our first baby. We had to meet with the community midwives for our area in case my appointed midwife is off duty for the birth and we collected some medical supplies from the hospital too. It seems so close now and I know all the hassles will seem a lifetime ago when the baby arrives.

I still find it hard to imagine what kind of person made it easier for someone to abandon their education and rely permanently on the state than to complete it (giving a much better chance of security in future) by removing the right to a few months' support. I'm just happy that we had the courage and the support to have made the right decision, to have our baby, in spite of this legislative discrimination. I hope anyone else who finds themselves faced with a similar situation will not let it discourage them.

61

'Things for your kids'

We did not get a lot of help, we could do better. Also we did not get a lot of money. We should get more money to help you buy things for your kids. You don't get a lot of help when you are pregnant. You should get more help when you have your kids.

62

'I just want to get my boys safely to adulthood'

I'm 35 years old and married with two sons aged nine and thirteen. We live in a Housing Association house and my husband works as a hospital storekeeper. When he comes home at tea time I go to work in the same hospital as an evening receptionist. This year we received a pay rise of less than £2 per week, our first for two years. The rent is due to go up by £4.70 per week this year.

Life is just one continuous struggle to make ends meet. My Child Benefit goes to top up my housekeeping and all my clothes come from Oxfam or jumble sales. Our one luxury is our D reg. car, which takes up a lot of our income, but without it we could not go anywhere as public transport is too expensive. We budget very carefully, putting aside money for bills each week. Sometimes we go wild and use the Access card to go to the pictures (about three times a year) or buy the kids shoes or clothes. Last year, my in-laws bought us an old but serviceable tent and we had several weekends away during the summer. There was little money so we took food with us. I save pennies and two pences to put in the building society for the boys to spend while we're away.

We both come from working-class families, so are used to making do, but we did hope that things would improve as the boys got older and I started part-time work. However, I now find that I really need more hours and could never give up work. We had to make sure we had no more children as we both feel it would be cruel to have a larger family on our income. When both boys are at secondary school, I hope to get daytime work and increase my hours and hopefully then we'll have more money, but I'm not happy about the idea of the boys being on their own for any length of time, as there are drug dealers in the area and I would be spending my working hours worrying about them. My mum is in her seventies and though she occasionally has my youngest son if I can get some overtime, she is not in good health and relies on me for company and help to go shopping, so I would feel guilty if I worked more hours and left her alone.

When I married I was a practising Catholic, but after fourteen years of marriage I have become increasingly disillusioned with my religion and find it impossible to live by its rules.

I just want to get my boys safely to adulthood and, if possible, to see them into college or employment. When they leave home, I hope my husband and I will be able to spend time together on outings and interests we can't afford now. However, when I see how my mum struggles on her pension and a small railway pension from my late father, I am not too hopeful.

63

'When I had a black eye . . . I would keep Lindsay off from playgroup'

I was first pregnant at the age of seventeen, a result of taking antibiotics whilst using the contraceptive pill. I hadn't been informed that antibiotics could reduce the pill's effectiveness. I was unmarried. My boyfriend and I decided to keep the baby – not a hard decision. I was working in a private home at the time as a nanny. I moved back in with my parents with my boyfriend. He was unable to marry me as he was going through divorce, even though he was only five years older. I did not want to get married, especially due to pregnancy. This was 1982. The hospital I was first booked into treated me with contempt. I changed hospitals when I moved back with my parents. The new hospital treated me extremely well. I was living in the West Midlands at the time. A locum consultant saw to me and gave me very special personal care due to my age and unmarried state. I would spend three hours at the hospital every time I had an appointment. This was normal for all pregnant women. We sat on hard-backed chairs and were treated like cattle. I was even forgotten about a number of times! The last six weeks I spent in and out of hospital. The consultant said the baby was too small. I would go in for a few days' rest and then come out again, only to go back in on my next appointment. I did feel extremely well. I felt the consultant worried unnecessarily.

The labour was painful but only lasted five and a half hours. I stayed five days in hospital. Once home I received no help. Although of course I only had Lindsay to see to. No housework, etc. Lindsay cried a lot. My boyfriend and mother just kept on saying 'She's hungry, feed her.' The house was cold. The visiting midwife had to tell my mother to put the heating on, even though my boyfriend had said he'd pay extra towards the heating. He had two weeks off work. He was on a government training scheme. Work was very understanding. Although my boyfriend had time off he didn't really do anything. He went drinking and smoked over the baby. My stitches were agony and the midwife said I should have called her out in the middle of the night. As if I would! She took my stitches out early.

Disposable nappies were incredibly expensive and hardly anyone used them. My mother believed that all baby's things should be hand washed. I had to lean over the bath washing baby things. Especially cot sheets. I found terry towelling nappies very unsatisfactory. The cot was soaked every morning. Lindsay got through a lot of nappies and clothes. I eventually gave up breast-feeding and gave Lindsay a dummy at one month old. We moved into our own rented house a couple of weeks later. I forgot to say that Lindsay was a normal birth and weighed 6 lbs 3 oz., not particularly small. I don't drink or smoke.

Money was very tight. My boyfriend eventually set up as a self-employed painter and decorator. He drank most of the money. He couldn't handle responsibility. We married when Lindsay was six months old. He desperately wanted to marry me. I gave in to pressure off my parents and him. He changed on the wedding night. I bitterly regret marrying him. But don't regret Lindsay. I got a little job cleaning a private house when Lindsay was nine months old. I took her with me. I will always be grateful to Susan for giving me that job. No references and she'd never seen me before. Straight away I had my own key. It was difficult taking Lindsay. But I earned £5 and desperately needed it. I bought little extras with the money for Lindsay. She had her clothes bought from Bewise and a lot were given to her secondhand. I got a second cleaning job when Lindsay was two years old, on the strength of Susan's reference. I had to use this money mostly to buy food. My husband behaved himself for six months and talked me into another baby. I did want another child and I wanted Lindsay to have a brother or sister. I also thought that I wanted my children to at least have the same father. Two weeks after having the positive pregnancy test, my husband decided he wanted rid of the baby. Because I refused, this was his reason for ignoring me and Lindsay for many months.

I had a trouble-free pregnancy. Although the hospital did start on saying the baby was too small. I told them they didn't know what they were on about. Leo was born 6 lb. 6 oz. His skin was very dark and his hair was jet black. Lindsay was blonde and very pink. Leo being dark was my husband's excuse to say he wasn't his. I wasn't interested in men. I worked up until a week before Leo was born, my stomach touching the floor when I was scrubbing.

When Leo was born I didn't cry, I wailed. I had desperately wanted a son. I cried for days with joy. I had to have an enema with Lindsay (hospital policy), not so with Leo. The whole experience was totally different, and much better. This was November 1985. I breast-fed Leo. I asked for help and was told I didn't need it as I'd already got one child. I had a lot of milk. My mother stayed with us until Leo was ten days old. When she went my husband demanded sex and punched me because I said I couldn't. I was breast-feeding at the time. The next morning my left breast was inflamed and I felt ill. I fainted in the shower. Lindsay found me. She, by the way, was a big help. I called the doctor out. He looked horrified when I produced my breast. He said there was nothing he could do and hastily left. I'm ashamed to say that I gave up breast-feeding. I really regret that. I had enjoyed feeding him and I had lots of milk. I know now that I had a breast infection.

Money was extremely tight. My husband went on the dole. He spent most of the day in bed. I telephoned my old employer and she was happy to have me back cleaning one morning a week. It was very hard and very tiring. Leo didn't sleep at night from when I was punched whilst feeding him. He used to sleep all day. Lindsay had always been very demanding. I felt life was very tiring. My health visitor was no support at all. My husband drank and smoked all night. I never knew where he was. I went down to seven stone. I was normally eight and a half stone. I managed to get my act together when my parents came up, usually once a week or fortnight. When Leo was four months old my husband beat me very badly. I managed to fend my parents off for a couple of weeks. I took Lindsay to playgroup. Usually when I had a black eye or such, I would keep Lindsay off from playgroup but this time I had hoped to slip in and out without being seen. The woman who ran it saw me. When I went to fetch Lindsay she spoke to me and sent me to another mum who dealt with battered women. For the first time I realized someone would believe me. These two women were the first who gave me support. The health visitor still didn't and the doctor just gave me the Marriage Guidance telephone number. My husband and I split up when Leo was six months old but got back together a few weeks later. My parents didn't believe I was being battered. Dad wanted evidence. I'd strived for months to conceal it from them so they wouldn't worry and be upset.

Lindsay got a horrible virus when she was four. She kept on coughing and being sick. There was a new doctor. Oh, he was so wonderful. So supportive. I practically lived in that surgery, convinced she was going to die. The doctor would always speak to me on the phone. He always saw me the minute I walked into the surgery. He talked to me and I could see light at the end of the tunnel. Lindsay started nursery school. They saw my black eyes. They were so supportive. They told me I didn't have to put up with it. I thought I did purely because I was married. I had a new health visitor, a man. He was supportive too. With all this support and the fact that my husband was now trying to force all sorts of kinky illegal sex on to me, regardless of the whereabouts of the children, I kicked him out.

Eventually in 1991 I met a wonderful, quiet, single man. I was 28 and he was 32. He has his own house and a good job. Me and the kids left our home and moved two miles away to his house. Being single, he wanted children. I never thought I'd have more children. We got married. My parents were pleased. My dad had stated that I should have worked harder at my marriage. They were ashamed of me being a single parent. Although they did help a lot with the children. I've never told them of the sexual side of my first marriage.

I was pregnant with Hannah Christmas 1991. My dad couldn't understand why I wanted more children and thought that my husband should be content with two 'ready mades'. I was in the Domino scheme to have Hannah. It was lovely. I took my children to parentcraft classes. The health visitor was lovely. My pregnancy was trouble-free. I was 21 hours in labour. My mum came to stay. I had no pain relief. My husband was with me throughout. Hannah was 7 lbs 5 oz. I requested that she be given to her dad first. I held her and just felt a quiet calm. She was his baby. I breast-fed. I asked for help and got it. To the point of the midwife holding my breasts and inserting the nipple properly into the baby's mouth. I fed Hannah successfully for four months. My antenatal appointments at the hospital were very friendly and efficient. I waited about ten minutes. I was in and out within half an hour. No one examined me internally and I was treated like a person. Even the chairs were comfortable. This was a hospital which has since closed down. I had to have a couple of stitches after having Hannah. I was petrified. It was a female nurse who saw to me. She was very kind and said to have a bit of gas and air. It was OK as it was a little tube that I had to suck through. The nurses left me alone with Hannah in a room next to the labour ward as she'd been born at midnight and they didn't want to disturb anyone on the wards. I was home by 10 a.m., just ten hours after having her. I felt really good, although very tired. When Hannah was two weeks old I had the same problem with my breast that I'd had with Leo. I felt very ill. I went to the doctor. I'd had to change doctors when we moved. He said I'd got an infection, gave me antibiotics and told me to call him out if I didn't feel better by evening. He recommended to put the baby to the breast to relieve the pressure. He was very good. Considering I hadn't had a lot to do with him, he was very nice and instantly gave me confidence in him. I thoroughly enjoyed breast-feeding Hannah.

My husband was very good. Although he had no urge to bath or change nappies he had always been a big help around the house. He washed up and sorted out washing and lots of other household things. I insisted on cooking tea the first night. My brother-in-law came round and was amazed. My mother was wonderful. She played with the other two, helped with their school work and took them to school, made tea, took the children out, did washing (everything in the machine in my house), did ironing, etc. I also did a lot, although admittedly most of my time was taken up breast-feeding. I fed the baby when she wanted it, which was nearly all the time. My mother stayed three weeks! None of us wanted her to go. She did say she'd fix it with work to stay longer, but I couldn't let her do that. Little things like having a shower, I felt I needed someone around. The baby always woke up when I stepped into the shower. In the event, I was fine. My husband had the first week off work. He spent a lot of the time asleep when I slept as he'd found it so exhausting.

My two older children were brilliant. They loved Hannah instantly. Lindsay bathed her every day (from day one). Leo played with her. My visiting midwife was brilliant. She'd seen to me all throughout the pregnancy. My health visitor was very nice and phoned when I had the breast infection.

There was plenty of money. Hannah didn't have all her equipment brand new, but clothes all were. She was in disposable nappies. That was one thing I was determined on. Ninety-nine per cent of people used disposable nappies. They were a godsend. No more messing about with Napisan and worrying about drying nappies. No way would I ever not use disposables again. I still made my own baby food as a personal preference. I registered as a childminder when Hannah was two years old. Mainly due to my love of children, but also because I wanted to earn money to make a contribution. My husband's been so good financially, so I'd like to make a contribution. Extra money always comes in handy, especially when you've got three children. When Lindsay was two years old, I spent a huge £30 on her. When Leo was two years old, I spent an enormous £50 on him. When Hannah was two years old we (note the we) spent £150 on her. I am able to buy things especially for Hannah – fromage frais, Quavers, grapes, special biscuits. I spend a lot on just food for her alone. She is quite small, but eats extremely well and is incredibly healthy. The other two were poor eaters, never had anything special and were frequently ill due to the cigarette smoke. Thank goodness they don't remember those days. They never went hungry though. But certainly never had the lovely food that Hannah has. They make up for it now though. They eat as much as my husband and I and are very healthy.

We have just moved to the seaside as my husband's work asked him if he'd consider it. The lifestyle is less hectic and the air fresher. My eldest is taking time to settle. I am in the process of registering for childminding as we all loved it so much in Birmingham.

64

'Mothers are thrown in at the deep end'

My name is Jenny, I am 37 years old and I have seven children. I have not worked in full-time employment since I married. Over the last three years I have had a couple of part-time jobs. I found the medical care with each of my children good, although I was not informed as to what was going on around me. I would not have asked those in the hospital any questions. If I did not ask I was told nothing.

The care I had after my children were born was not so good. The more children I had, the less after-care I received. I was told the reason for this was that I was able to cope as I had plenty of experience because I had so many children. I think the after-care when you have had a baby is very important, as many mothers come home from the hospital and are thrown in at the deep end, cleaning, cooking, washing, looking after the other children, and not all mothers can cope. There has been a step backwards in the care after the birth of your baby.

'We were in a b. & b.'

Hi, Dolly here! When I was pregnant we were in a b. & b. [bed and breakfast]. Konrad's father wouldn't give me any money so I had to steal it. I had it bad, I was in a horrible relationship with Konrad's father, he used to hit me and make me sleep on the floor. I was never allowed out of the house, he was a pig. I had sickness all day, I had heartburn too. We could not afford fresh fruit or vegetables. Konrad's father would not allow me to have the milk tokens, he'd have them for eggs.

When Konrad was born it went from bad to worse. My giving birth was a nightmare. I didn't know what had hit me, I thought I was going to die before he came out. It felt as though I was fighting for my life, I could hear everything around me, then it went black, then light, a big light, it was beautiful indeed to be in the light and then you wake up ready to push, then Konrad was born. He was so beautiful and he was mine, all mine, he was so bonny. When you've had a child you feel empty, a weird empty, etc. A few months later I got my first house. I had nothing, bringing a baby into a world of hell. Okay, I had a grant from the DSS [Department of Social Security] but these days it doesn't go far. Everything I have has been given to me. Money doesn't go far now, it really hurts this year, my kids have to go without for Xmas because I can't afford to buy them anything. I feel really guilty but I can't do anything about it. They are the only reason I'm still alive because I love them so much and no one will ever change that. They are my life in 24 years, what a life. I could go on and on but I don't think you'd like to hear about it.

'My old office skills were outdated'

I am a divorcee who lived on Income Support from September 1990 to October 1994. My marriage had ended, I had a young daughter to care for, and my old office skills were outdated. Originally I had tried to go out to work but met various problems. The two main ones were the ongoing problem of suitable, affordable child care. My daughter was at school, which actually was harder to arrange care for. I have a mortgage and the interest rates were high. With the skills I had, I couldn't get a job which paid enough to cover all my outgoings. Being on benefit teaches you a whole new set of skills: stretching cash to buy shoes for your child and pay the gas bill; negotiating payment dates for bills; spotting good clothes in different corners, and surviving on a diet which concentrates on not being hungry rather than being healthy.

The whole process grinds you down. Every day is a struggle to balance all the demands on you. During this time I have had bouts of depression brought on by all the stress of the situation. These have required medical care although I have fortunately been able to care for my daughter throughout. Obviously this hasn't been easy for either of us. I have no family, my parents died when I was a child, so I am quite literally on my own. I've involved myself with voluntary work in the past, it helps to keep your own problems in perspective. Children don't see things in the same way and although my daughter is wonderful and rarely complains, she obviously envies her friends with their holidays, brand-name clothes, etc. Even having a friend round to tea can put a strain on an already overstretched budget.

One of my worst financial moments came when I came off benefit and on to a student grant. The Child Support Agency had been collecting my maintenance from my ex-husband and sending it to the Benefits Agency. They continued to do this despite several letters and phone calls from me and the Benefits Agency informing them of my change of circumstances. This situation was only resolved when I contacted my MP, who dealt direct with the CSA and resolved the problem for me. This whole process had taken three months. My grant had been calculated taking my maintenance into account. Having previously been on benefit I had no money put aside for such emergencies. It was a very difficult time when I was coping with a lot of new circumstances in my life. Now I'm a student studying for a degree in Behavioural Science and looking to the future. The only good point about the years on benefit is it's been a great training for living on a student grant!

'We are moving out'

I have three children; two are boys and one is a girl. Ages are eight years, eighteen months and eight weeks. It's very difficult to sort out the two babies at the moment. Throughout my pregnancies I ate well, but now I have no time. I mainly carried the girl better than I carried the boys. I'm getting very tired because of the way she (the baby) is – very demanding with her feeding and I'm getting tired quicker. I won't be having any more children as I have been sterilized now at the young age of 28, the reason being in past pregnancies I've lost so many. I lost two identical twins at three weeks in 1991. All my babies were small. Now I've had my three, I don't need any more.

My Mark's been good with the kids, he does help out with them both. He hasn't been able to get a steady job. It's a struggle living on Income Support. The house is too small for us now with three kids. It's impossible to get a good night's sleep. I can't move the bed down into the living room. Where are we supposed to eat? On our laps? So I've had enough of London. We are moving out. It's no good for the kids here. I'm fed up with all the arguments with the housing people. That's it really.

68

'The love a baby brings'

I am a 30-year-old working mother with a three-year-old daughter and a new baby. My husband is a plate layer and works away from home 90 per cent of the time. He is 38 years old. A woman today is expected to be a wife, mother and a worker bringing in the second wage. It is hard enough cleaning house and looking after your children without outside work, but it can be achieved if you have help. After having my second baby, which I had at home and would recommend to any healthy woman, I had to learn to step back and accept help to do everyday things, like cleaning, ironing and washing, thanks to my husband who took time from his work and my mother who helped every day until I could manage myself. I got into a routine with my two children and could add, slowly, outside work as well.

Juggling all these things can make you feel you can't cope. I know I am lucky having support from my family and this has made a big difference in my recovery. I am back to normal now and ready to enjoy the love a baby brings to all my family, especially me.

'I refuse to be broken-spirited'

My name is Bashiru and I am a Jamaican, thrice-married, divorced and now single person and parent of six children. I currently have a partner and we have been together five years but things are a bit shaky between us at the moment. I am on Income Support although I go to college one day a week and am hoping to go back to university in September. I am 39 years old (40 in November) but feel sixteen years old still! My children comprise four girls and two boys which is an even balance for me as I have a special preference, rightly or wrongly, for girl children. The age range is twenty, fourteen, eleven, eight and a half and six and a half years, plus the new addition who is just two weeks old.

I have always been on my own. I believe throughout having these children I somehow cannot seem to sacrifice my life to irresponsible men who are supposed to be fathers. So I have always worked and studied and am trained as a counsellor, a trainer, completed one and a half years of my degree which I changed twice and am looking to change again for September. Having the children has never been a major setback for me, except that I have wanted to return to Jamaica for a long time but finances obviously won't allow. That's not been because I have children, it's about the lack of financial support and otherwise from their fathers.

Now I have the baby I am continuing my one-day-a-week certificated course in HIV/AIDS and sexual health, two hours a week teaching drama and storytelling skills to young black children and looking, maybe, for another part-time or full-time job (if it's worth it) and returning to my degree in September. I have to sort out child care and am in the process of doing that too. Hopefully I can get a nursery place either at college, university or council depending of course on my eligibility. We presently live in council accommodation, a maisonette with three bedrooms, and I have tried to get a transfer to larger accommodation, but because of arrears cannot seem to succeed. That has been very frustrating in its own way, but I accept it from the point of view that I am more or less comfortable where I am for the time being and hate moving anyway!! My Income Support is £66 per week which is nothing to brag about, but the Lord provides, that is my faith and I have proven that in my life. The fact that we are not starving and have shelter, clothes, etc. means there is a force stronger than the DSS [Department of Social Security] and that is God in whom I find strength. So to hell with the DSS and others who feel they can break my will and that of many others. Where there is a will there must be a way and I have often found ways of surviving. Of course this does not change the fact that I believe there needs to be an improvement in welfare benefits. It's just that so far I refuse to be broken-spirited and find ways of getting on with the process of living which is gone in the blink of an eye. I love life and living and the hopes which can sometimes become a reality if you want them to and being a mother of six children gives me even more impetus to achieve what could be seen as impossible for someone with my status. I may be down a little financially but my spirit is very much alive and well and my lively, kind-hearted, sometimes exasperating children are also an inspiration to me, themselves and others.

'The Social will take them'

I lost my [benefits] book. I have had nothing since February. They say that the book has been cashed up to August. Social will not backdate to the beginning when I lost my book, not even the milk tokens. I am unable to live on it.

I work, part-time, escort work, anything available at the time! Difficult to get hold of the book to get a new one. Proof of pregnancy sent twice, both lost. Won't chase it up because of the Social/police. Don't get anywhere. Nowhere to live. Living on the floor of a friend's room. How can I bring up twins there? The Social will take them.

'A fraction above the poverty line'

I am 24 years old, a psychology student and married. At the moment I am not working as I want to spend the first year with my baby and then plan to continue with my psychology degree. My husband is presently unemployed so we have to rely on state benefits to survive and compared to what mothers in the early 1900s had to cope with, the help that mothers, single and married, receive now is better. However, the money that mothers on Income Support are entitled to before and after childbirth is purely only issued to keep them a fraction above the poverty line.

The amount before childbirth is approximately £36 per week. With that you need to stock up on baby items which are very expensive. Not only are there baby items to consider, but the items needed by the mother during pregnancy and afterwards. Nowadays it is standard policy to award an expectant mother with £100 but only if she is in receipt of Income Support. What about the mothers-to-be who are not claiming benefits, but who are living on insufficient funds? Furthermore, to be able to claim a Community Care Grant it seems there needs to be a major catastrophe, e.g. the house falling down, before it is even considered. Therefore state benefits for pregnant women, I have to say, are insufficient, and also state benefits after childbirth are just the same, because a mother (single) is expected to live on approximately £77 per week. When you consider the price of nappies, baby clothes, equipment, food, bills, etc. the money does not stretch very far.

On to the subject of antenatal care. Personally I found my

antenatal care from the midwives fantastic. I never met such helpful and supportive people in my life. However, care from my GP was diabolical. He was so interested in getting the appointments over in the space of one minute that he left himself unapproachable in the sense of discussing problems or fears. As for postnatal care, again the hospital and community midwives were brilliant, but I was surprised to find out that they (community midwives) had to stop visiting me after the tenth day due to cost cuts. This in itself resulted in me giving up breast-feeding, because I did not have the support I needed at a very crucial time.

72

'. . . Because of the bankruptcy agreement'

I am a teacher, my partner a civil structural engineer, and we have a seven-year-old son, Alan. My son was born when I was 36 years old. I attended all the antenatal classes laid on by the NCT [National Childbirth Trust] up until the last month when my high blood pressure forced me into hospital. Alan was induced at 37 weeks and he had a poor birth weight, just over 5 lbs. Jessops Hospital for Women in Sheffield looked after us both very well. There was no family anywhere near us; I relied heavily on the friends I had made in the NCT and established a supportive network. My home help, who had had thirteen children of her own, gave me lots of advice. I really didn't have a clue. I had always been a 'career girl', hence leaving it so late to have Alan. I actually think 36 is too late to start having children. I had two miscarriages (at 38 and 39) and failed to produce a brother or sister for Alan. This is difficult for me to come to terms with because I was one of four. My partner and I both desperately try to over-compensate for this by providing maximum 'quality time' for Alan – poor kid! Exhausting for us, and probably trying for him! I returned to work part-time when Alan was seven months old. Getting good child care is not easy. At two years he attended a lovely Montessori nursery. My own mother was not 'allowed' by her husband to work during the years she was bringing us up – and indeed afterwards – and this fact made me determined that I would never end up in the same situation. She was a bright, sensitive, intelligent woman who suffered severe mental damage coping with the situation she was placed in.

When Alan was born in 1987 my partner's business was thriving, but then, in the 'post-Thatcher economy', things went very wrong. We almost lost our house, the business failed, and the burden of 'making ends meet' fell on my shoulders. I had previously regarded teaching as a vocation rather than a money-making exercise. In fact we cannot even sell our house at the present time, because of the bankruptcy agreement. We are still having to pay this expensive mortgage and attendant bills, even though we would like to be in a smaller house with less financial commitment. We are no longer able, of course, to afford a home help. I had to sell my car and buy a cheaper one, paying for it through extended payments. I started going round the jumble sales and secondhand-clothes shops for Alan and me. It's no shame when you realize half the world is doing it.

It was difficult to provide a nutritious and balanced menu for Alan. Also, we had looked into the possibility of sending him to an independent school and had been round them, but we had to put him into a state infants' school, which is actually very good. My husband went through a long period of depression and perhaps when things get bad, on a bad day, I could blame him but I try not to, to keep the peace and family situation going. I think that what has happened has brought tension into our relationship. This is always there. But we've tried hard to do our best to make sure Alan has not been affected adversely. I feel I am constantly juggling with my life trying to be a mother, a teacher, a painter, a home-maker and a wife. Although my partner is very helpful with Alan and in the home, I still feel that the ultimate responsibilities for Alan's happiness, security and health are mine.

I have tremendous admiration for other mothers – the bond of motherhood is very strong. It is such a struggle to keep going on 'all cylinders'. God knows how they managed without Pampers and convenience foods a generation ago! I worry about the role of women in the future. How can we possibly be expected to cope with everything and do it all?

73

'Branded a druggie single mother'

Watching my daughter play and learn brings great pleasure to me as it does to many mothers. Being a single pregnant woman on Income Support made me realize how much the government despises us and makes it impossible to enjoy pregnancy or birth. I needed to be housed, I was living in a bed and breakfast. Before the council had given me a place to stay, they had demanded the names and numbers of my friends and family. They had then proceeded to phone them and ask why I couldn't live with them. They even phoned my parents in the USA and asked them.

At my antenatal clinic I had been asked if I'd ever taken drugs in the past. I told them I'd taken Ecstasy years before my pregnancy and that I'd smoked cannabis for years. This was written on my report. They asked me if I took any drugs now. I told them I didn't even smoke cigarettes. In the seventh month of pregnancy I was asked if I'd take a drug test. I said yes, I didn't mind. A week later I was told that the drug methadone was found in my urine. I was devastated when I realized that they did not believe me when I denied it, because I'd done drugs earlier in my life. I was single, black, pregnant and they weren't going to let any of the stereotypes the media had placed on us pass me by. I was branded a druggie single mother. I had to sit through meetings with social workers telling me how my baby was going to suffer withdrawal after birth. I went through this period of my pregnancy in a daze. I couldn't believe what was happening to me. I wanted this baby so much. It was this want that got me through. I told them I'd never taken methadone before. I was ignored. The test showed positive and that was it. I fell into every labelled box they'd ever tried to shove me in.

The day after my beautiful daughter was born I discharged myself from hospital and went to stay with my sister. I was so frightened my daughter would be taken away. My daughter developed jaundice on the third day and had to go back in for a few tests. While I was there my hospital social worker came over, she was all smiles, she told me my urine had been contaminated (accidentally??) and that they wanted to apologize. As I walked away one thing she said kept repeating itself, 'You must be so relieved.'

74

'Every working mother's dream'

I am 32 years old and have two children aged eight and six years. I have worked all my life, since leaving secretarial college at seventeen. I started a family when I was 24 years old and gave up full-time work to look after my children, although I continued to work part-time. Both my children are now at primary school and I work during the school hours (9.30 a.m. to 3.00 p.m.). If I have to work late, I rely on my mother (who lives near me) to collect the children from school and look after them until I get home. This works OK until it comes to the school holidays and half-terms. I use a private playscheme during the holidays, which the children love going to, but it obviously works out expensive having to pay for two children. My wages are only part-time (I work as a bookkeeper) but to cover my hours the cost of the playscheme is over £1,000 a year. It works out that about £22 a week of my net income is spent on holiday playschemes alone! If I had to pay for after-school care when I worked late, it would obviously be costing even more, and bearing in mind my work is only part-time, it is a large chunk out of my wages.

The thing I resent most about paying for child care is that there is no tax relief whatsoever for working mothers. I wouldn't expect to get tax relief for paying a neighbour or friend to look after my children, but a registered playscheme should be different. I know there are some benefits for mothers on Income Support to claim child care, but there are lots of women like myself who are just above that category of income and miss out. My husband is a mechanic and fairly low-paid. In fact, if I didn't work we would qualify for Family Credit, but I choose to work because I am capable of working and it still brings in a bit more than relying on Family Credit, but because of it I miss out on the only benefits for working mothers. I don't resent the benefits given to low-income mothers, but working mothers, like myself, should be allowed to claim tax relief on the payments to registered playschemes and nurseries. I apologize if I'm getting on my soap box and moaning about one subject only. But all the time we hear about women being encouraged to return to work, but in reality we get no help whatsoever. Tax relief isn't much to ask – especially when by working we are not only saving the government money in benefits we could claim from the state but quite the reverse, we are contributing National Insurance contributions and income tax!

I will finish here with my comments on being a working mother, rather than fill lots more pages about the difficulties of making ends meet (yes – a big problem). Much as I enjoy my job, I still feel guilty about not having enough time for the children, because when we all get home I have to start on my other job (unpaid) of cooking, cleaning, washing, etc., and getting everything ready for school and work the next day. I sometimes think it would be nice if we were better off financially, so I didn't have to work the hours I do. Then I'd do all the housework during the day and be able to spend lots of time with the children after school – every working mother's dream!

'My husband was diagnosed as having mental problems'

I had my first child at the age of 25 years. I married my husband when I was 22. The second child came along at least seven years after the first. I was a machinist before marriage working in Wolverhampton, and when I came to London I carried on for a while working at home and looking after my son. I stopped working as a machinist after my second child. My husband was then working and bringing in a fair wage.

Unfortunately three years ago my husband was diagnosed as having mental problems. He was admitted to a mental institution, he is currently in a home. He has changed from being a bubbly and cheerful person to a poor and almost lifeless person. He does recognize the children but he cannot do anything for them. He cannot play with them as before and he appears to have lost touch with reality. He is often on drugs to calm him down.

Since he became ill my oldest son has had real problems. He is difficult, uncooperative, always in trouble. He has changed more than three schools just this year. He argues with me constantly, lies, disappears for hours on end, fights with his sister regularly. He can however be helpful around the house, shopping, etc. The little one is slowly picking up some of his habits. There are times when I feel sad, lonely, desperate and ready to give all up. But I have supportive friends and family and they keep me going. The kids see their father regularly at the home. I work as an administrator, after managing to do a HND [Higher National Diploma] course and get a good wage. So all in all I am fine and keep praying that the children will grow out of their difficulties.

'I would prefer to work part-time'

I am 36 years of age and have two children aged two and four. My husband is a foreman at a large engineering company and I work full-time as a secretary. If I had a choice, I would prefer to work part-time but our current finances do not enable me to do so. Before I commenced maternity leave, I managed to save some money for the months when I received no salary or maternity pay, which did help considerably. However, if I had not been able to do this we would have struggled. I found it very hard returning to work after enjoying my months at home with both children and wished that I could have stayed off longer. I would have liked to have spent the time with them prior to nursery school, or at least their first two years, before returning to work but had I done this I would have found it extremely difficult to find a job as convenient and well-paid as the one I have.

The first six months after returning to work from having my second child were hard in that I found it difficult to manage a full-time job and run a home whilst looking after my family. However, as time went on I realized that it is impossible to do everything when you're working and some jobs just have to be put off as my main priority is the children and my time spent with them is precious.

'The "deserving" and "undeserving" poor'

Although I now enjoy a reasonably comfortable lifestyle, ten years ago the picture was very different. At the time I was married and my child was aged four. My marriage was deteriorating rapidly, my husband was extremely hostile and verbally abusive to me nearly all the time and was very resentful that I had given up my job as a nurse to take a social science degree at the local polytechnic. I had a grant of about £3,500 at the time and had to pay nursery fees as well as contributing to the mortgage of our flat (owned in his name). The situation deteriorated so much that I became very afraid for my safety and felt that it was impossible to bring up my little girl in this atmosphere. My brother and his partner lived nearby and offered to put me and my daughter up if I had the courage to leave. I did so, and started trying to negotiate to get myself rehoused (my husband completely refused to consider leaving the flat).

Living on a student grant in North London, I was unable to afford any commercial rent and I approached the local council. Despite the fact that I was living in a one-bedroom flat, which meant that my daughter and myself were sleeping in the living room which obviously put a strain on the couple, I apparently did not have enough points to be entitled to council housing. I applied to numerous housing associations and eventually was given an interview by the Peabody Trust. Their criteria for need very much echoed the 'deserving' and 'undeserving' poor categories that I was learning about in my social policy lectures, and I was informed that I was not considered to be 'deserving' for the following reasons: I was intentionally homeless as I had left my husband; although my income was undoubtedly very low at the time, the acquisition of a degree would mean that I had the potential to eventually acquire a reasonable job; and that as I was perceived as 'articulate and middle class' I would stand a better choice of being rehoused in other ways. Whereas I can sympathize with this view to a certain extent, it was extremely demoralizing and unhelpful to me at the time. Although I did eventually, after six months and much effort on my part, get rehoused in a shared-housing scheme, this was an extremely stressful and distressing time, often compounded by the treatment of housing officials.

'Both of us live in one room'

My son is now eight months (he is called Jacob) and both of us live in one room on little more than £70 a week. I live with another single mum who has two older boys. She rents me the room. I thought that the stigma associated with single parents had gone, but through personal experience I found that it is still attached. I didn't become pregnant or single by choice but I love my son just as much as any mother in marriage or a relationship. I hope that more people finally admit that the way we are forced to live is hard and yes – we do have to make sacrifices if our children need clothes or shoes.

'There is no money for luxuries'

I have five children, aged from eleven years to three months. I'm married, my husband is working and we don't claim any state benefits, except Child Benefit. But that doesn't make us rich. In fact, until my husband's last pay rise, we actually received £50 per month less than we needed for bills. When my eldest was little, I used to work, as my husband had very low-paid jobs. Unfortunately as the companies he worked for were paying for him to study for professional qualifications, they paid him very poorly, but it was always just above Income Support level. When I worked, all but £10 of my money went to the childminder. When my second child was born, it just wasn't worth working during the school holidays, as I had to pay full rate for both her and my son. Reluctantly, I gave up work when she was six months old. Since then, I've had a few part-time evening jobs, but they haven't been very satisfactory. I had one job whilst pregnant with my fourth child at a petrol station. I was the only person on the site until eight o'clock at night. I spent the winter months in absolute terror of an armed attack, as three petrol stations in the area were held up in the space of a few months. In the end I was asked to leave – not from any concern for my safety, but because my pregnancy had started to show and it made the garage a 'plum target'.

At the moment, I can't work in the evenings as my husband now works in Maidenhead and doesn't reach home until 6.15 p.m. I swear, practically every job in this area starts at 6 p.m. The only exception is Sainsburys which runs a 7–11 p.m. shift. It's just such a late finish for a woman with children. It can be midnight before you're home and wound down ready for bed. It only takes one child to wake in the night, and you're a zombie by the time 5.30 a.m. and breakfast comes.

Ideally, I'd like to work for a couple of hours in the day, but it's almost impossible. All the back-to-work incentives seemed to be aimed at single mums. There is just no affordable child care for anybody with two children or more. So, I'm stuck at home with three children under school age – having to pay for the three-year-old's nursery school because I'm not on benefits. Because I can't work, there's no money for luxuries. We haven't had a holiday in nine years, yet a single mother of my acquaintance had three last year, all paid for by various agencies designed to ease the stress of single parents. I don't feel enough is done to support those of us who support the economy with our taxes. We are by no means 'middle income', but neither are we in the poverty trap. We are just abandoned by every government initiative, left to struggle on as best we can, only of interest on Budget Day when the Chancellor of the day slaps a bit more duty on to petrol and decides to freeze Child Benefit once again, as we probably don't need it as we're not collecting a means-tested benefit. I'm a working mother, working damned hard at home to bring up the next generation and I can tell you, the help I get is bugger all!

80

'The caring, loving support of a husband named J'

I have three children aged between one and a half and twelve and a half. Married now, I was a single mum with my oldest, M. I was raped when I was twelve years old and from that day on I was on every major tranquillizer and I was under the Social Work Department. I had a lot of people in my life, I did not cope, everybody else did it for me. It was hard being mother and father. I would play with M on the floor and the next thing I knew I would be waking up. I lost so much of my life because of drugs and so much of motherhood with M. Things went from bad to worse. Consistency was very hard. One day I let M get away with something and the next day I would shout at her. My worse thing was M and I were of the same nature and would rub each other up.

I went into a psychiatric hospital a couple of times. That's when things came to a head. M went to her granny's (her father's mother). I was not to get her back. Then she went to my dad. That caused a lot of heartache and I said a lot of things which I was so sorry for to my late dad. Then I met another man who was bringing up a girl on his own too, but the social workers thought it was a bad thing for us to be together. So that ended. I met someone while in hospital but that was another bad thing because the two of us were on drugs prescribed by the doctor. So that ended. I lost a lot of self-confidence and started to believe I was the person the Social Work Department said I was. Then I met my husband.

By this time M was in care with my dad. He took ill and had

to go into hospital. So with my dad out the road they (social workers) went the full road. I must say when I went into hospital I was told I would get M back when my dad came back out of hospital. M was in temporary foster care. I could not see M at all, it would do more harm than good, they said. I never hit my wee girl. I had a clean home. But being on so many tablets, life was one big blur. M went into long-term foster care. A local charity got me a lawyer. She was good but the Social Work Department decided M was to go for closed adoption. I was never to see M again. My family was not to see M, not anyone. When on all these tablets I was a manic depressive for years, the doctors said. I think someone should have sat down and spoken to me after being raped, but mum and dad kept it quiet and I was told to get on with life. I lost a child to J, my husband now, because of all the carry-on with the Social Work. But J put all my tablets down the toilet. I did not really think I was taking bad withdrawals because I was too busy thinking of losing M.

M had her eighth birthday party in the house. It was to be her last. Social Work asked me to do a life-story book with M but I never gave up. J and I were expecting our first child. M was told she would never see her wee brother or sister. I was in hospital at about six or seven months pregnant. Out of the blue – after Social Work had said that M was not coming home – I was told that she was coming home for rehabilitation. I could not believe it. All this time not seeing M or having her with us and all of a sudden she was coming home. It was a long process but she did come home and is still home five years later. When we were told M was coming home we went to a panel and walked away with M and no social worker. A bit hard to believe after going for closed adoption.

I am still trying to piece bits of my life together. I had lost so many years when I came off my tablets. I had to learn to crawl before I could walk. I had really bad panic attacks but I am more in control of my life now. The funny thing is I now go and speak to mothers for the breast-feeding promotion project on the estate and give them support. I've got my First Aid and passed my driving test. And I was the very one who helped my social worker when she had really bad personal problems, the very one who said a leopard cannot change their spots. I have changed but not with help from doctors and social workers but from the caring, loving support of a husband named J.

81

'I only needed a basket and never a trolley'

I was nineteen when I first fell pregnant. My husband was in the Forces and getting ready to go on a tour for six months. We were living in army quarters in England. I moved back to Scotland a month before my baby was due so I could be with my own family, and also I wanted my baby to be Scottish. My first child (a boy) was born exactly a week late. That week felt like a month. It was a great relief knowing that he was healthy and that I had the support of my family when I got out of hospital, as my husband was by now somewhere in the middle of America. It took him a week to find out that he had a son and he saw him for the first time when he was four and a half months old.

My second child (another boy) was born five days early. The birth was a lot easier for me but it seemed to be more complicated for the nurses and they eventually brought someone else in who mentioned the word 'forceps'. This gave me a fright and I remember pushing him out before they got a chance to use them. Again I had a healthy boy but I was told he was a girl. My husband was at the birth this time and he told me later on in the ward that he was sure it was a boy. I was not convinced until he checked inside his nappy and I saw for myself. There is just one and a half years between the boys. Two years later I had my third (a girl). Again my husband was on tour and did not see her until a month later. She was so different from the boys. My eldest has black hair, the second has red hair and she had blonde hair. This eventually fell out and she now has red hair like her brother. Her birth was the hardest. She was born in Germany and I did not have any drugs or gas and air, etc. Everything was there if I needed it but I chose not to. The nurse was with me all the time and she was great. When the baby's head came out she asked me if I wanted a mirror to see. I said no but now I wish I had. After my third child I decided there would be no more children.

Three years later I divorced my husband and became a single parent. At that time the children were aged six and a half, five and three. We had everything we needed in our council house and when my husband left he only took his personal belongings and a hi-fi and TV with him. So when I first went on Income Support at least I had a good start. My neighbour was also a single parent so she warned me how difficult things would be. The hardest bit at the beginning was getting used to having all the money on a Monday (Income Support and Child Benefit) and knowing it had to last a full week. At least when my husband was with me I had my Child Benefit on the Monday and wages on Friday. I think Income Support should be paid on a Thursday or Friday as well. Things didn't seem too bad at the start, I got used to a lower income and learnt quickly to buy stamps for phone, electric and gas bills. I had to miss out on a few luxuries and I gave up my catalogue [mail order], but I seemed to be coping fine.

Then I received a letter from Social Security. I had to go and see them. In the office the man said that by mistake I had been getting paid for six children on my book instead of three. I was now due them over £100. I honestly didn't know about this and the man said it was OK but it had to be paid back at £2.50 a week. By the time I had my book renewed, the £2.50 deducted and the 'extra three children' payment taken off (nearly £30), I realized that things really were going to be hard. At least I didn't pay rent although I couldn't manage it anyway. I became depressed, lack of money was a nightmare, in one hand and out the other at the post office. I stopped buying newspapers and read my neighbour's instead. I hardly ever used the phone and when I did the conversation was short. My mum made me put the phone down when

I called her and she would ring me straight back to save my bill. I felt out of touch with normal living. I never went downtown unless I had to. I hated walking round the shops knowing that I couldn't afford much. I never used the bus. Before I was short of money I sometimes bought things in charity shops, but knowing that I had to shop there was making me feel miserable. I had to total up my shopping at the supermarket before I reached the check-outs. Even knowing that I only needed a basket and never a trolley for the few daily items I bought made me feel miserable, especially when you see other people's stacked full. Seeing children with nice clothes and expensive trainers made me jealous. I wished I could buy these things for my kids. I shouted a lot more at my kids than I used to. They were always asking for things and I was always saying I couldn't afford it.

Before I would think nothing of having a family tea from the chip shop, renting out a video or going to the corner shop for a loaf of bread and some 'goodies'. Now I was turning up the telly at a certain time every night so the kids wouldn't hear the ice-cream van coming, I was rummaging for clothes at jumble sales and most of my shopping was from the reduced corner at the supermarket. Every Saturday or Sunday we went to my mum's. This was the best time of the week. The kids could eat what they wanted and I always got food to take home with me for later. If it wasn't for my parents I don't know how I would have coped. The school holidays were the best time of the year. Although I spent more on food we all went out to pick berries. I knew this was not allowed as far as my benefits were concerned but it was worth the risk. I used to make about £15 a day. I'd keep £5 for the daily shopping and the extra got spent on presents for Christmas. The kids made their own money for sweets and comics so they were happy and so was I.

I had no social life apart from visiting my neighbours. All my neighbours were great but I didn't feel at ease with some of them when they started talking about holidays they'd been on, or new clothes they'd bought, even when they talked about the pub at the weekends. I felt so out of touch. Sitting in their houses with a cup of coffee they would always bring out a cake or chocolate biscuits, etc. I knew I couldn't keep up with doing the same when they came to my house, so although I remained good friends with them all I stopped visiting them and just went to the one neighbour who like myself was a single parent. At least we both knew what each other was going through and our conversations were on the same wavelength. Things eventually got a bit easier again, I finished paying off the £2.50 and even that seemed like a bonus. After a year on Income Support the money also went up, not by much but it was still a big help. The first year is definitely the worst until you get yourself into a routine, especially if you've been used to having a husband or partner who worked. Most people are great and don't look down on you but that doesn't stop you feeling low about yourself.

I eventually got a part-time job childminding then I carried on to be a foster parent. I started to have a social life again and met a nice man. I got sterilized after I was divorced but a year and a half later I asked the doctor if he would reverse it. My local hospital said no, so I asked the family doctor if he would refer me to the next hospital. This hospital didn't object but told me there was a nine-month waiting list. About ten months later I had the operation to repair my tubes. Two weeks after that I was pregnant again. I had another healthy boy. The age gap between him and my eldest is just over twelve years. I have no intentions of having any more children so I have 'norplant' in my arm which lasts five years. I would never marry again but I am quite happily living with my fiancé whom I've been with for eight years. I hope I never end up on Income Support again but at least I know how hard it is.

82

'It doesn't get easier
but you get used to it'

When I had my first child I had been unemployed for six months and my husband was a student. Money was very tight and we managed off a grant. We lived in a one-bed council flat and assumed we would get a rent rebate since we lived on a low income. So we stopped paying rent thinking it would be reduced. Thinking about it now it was a silly thing to do because we found out that since my husband was a student we didn't qualify for a rent rebate and we had to repay all the back-rent (about three months by the time the council had got around to dealing with our application). So the last of our savings had gone. When the baby arrived everyone was very generous buying items and I received lots of second-hand things. But (and it may sound a bit ungrateful) I did feel like a charity case – I couldn't buy anything and we relied on hand-outs. Friends of friends would pass on baby clothes – which was nice – but I longed to buy his first pair of shoes or his first winter coat.

When you live on a restricted income for long enough you do become used to the lifestyle – it doesn't get easier but you get used to it. I didn't go window shopping because it brought home the fact that I couldn't buy anything.

I once went to an open farm with my toddler thinking it was free to get in – to my horror it wasn't. I just had enough to pay for the entrance. I didn't want to have to borrow the money from my friends. After the farm when they were all tucking into scones and tea, having the excuse of being 'on a diet' was handy – rather than admit I couldn't even afford a cup of tea.

My baby was born in July 1987, the year the government abolished payments for maternity items and the Maternity Grant. Later the rules changed for help for students. There was so little help available for us. We were both 30 years old, my husband was studying so he could improve his work prospects, and I didn't want to wait any longer to have my first child. These were planned decisions and we expected some hardship for several years but thought that we could expect some state help. After all, we fully expected that at some time in the future we would be working and our tax and National Insurance contributions would go to help someone else in that position.

'Most working women I know work for the money, not for the career'

I think the media has the wrong idea of working women. Most working women I know work for the money, not for the career. They also work part-time and rarely have expectations to further their careers. I have read so many articles in the 'glossy' magazines which talk about nannies, and careers – they seem to look at the exception rather than the rule. The media also gives the impression that women are working for their independence, when in reality it is to support their families.

'Too far for my mum to travel'

At the age of 27 I had my first and only child in 1989. As with more modern mums, after thirteen weeks I returned to work and had the wonderful advantage of having my mum as a full-time carer for my daughter. As my mum is a widow, I paid her for her time by paying her gas and electricity bills along with a bus pass as she hasn't a car. The rough total was £70 per month. At the time I was in a well-paid job and didn't miss the money. After three years due to moving house it became too far for my mum to travel so I made arrangements to have my daughter cared for by a childminder. She takes her to school and collects her and gives her a meal until I pick her up after work. This arrangement is fine but costly. I pay her £140 a month and half as a retainer in the holidays if you don't use her services, or £2 per hour if you do use her services – to me £20-plus per day. Also I have moved jobs due to redundancy and have had to accept lower pay as a result.

'Well, I agree the benefit barely covers these . . .'

I am a single parent with three children, twelve years and twins of six years. Quite honestly it makes me very mad to watch these programmes on TV that harp on about how poor every single parent on benefits (of which I am one) is. The presenters make a good job of getting the public's sympathy and the parents themselves decry their lot over and over again. Do they really believe the government should pay for them to go out and have a good time, smoke and drink, play bingo, etc. etc? They moan they cannot feed their children – do they expect to feed them steak or/and joints of best beef?

Right, well, you probably think I'm speaking out of turn by now. I get £76 per week Social money. I get about £22 per week Child Benefit, £12 per week maintenance. That's for all of us = £110 per week. I get my mortgage interest paid to the building society. I have £13 per week gross to find and pay to the building society myself. I have gas, electric, water, phone, TV licence, life insurance, contents insurance to find the same as everybody else. Then I have to clothe and feed us. Well, I agree that the benefit barely covers these, but with good management one can do it. Albeit there is nothing to spare for the pleasures mentioned above. Especially holidays, which we have never had since the twins were born. But I don't expect it. Why should the government pay for these things when they had no hand in me getting pregnant! It's bad enough having to rely on Social Security for the bare necessities. And we have everything we need and me and the children feed well and are clothed well.

I could say a lot more but I think you should have got the message – here's one single parent who has what she needs, and the greatest gift of all – love of a family.

P.S. I am a state-enrolled nurse. The reason I don't work is because I cannot get child care to cover the shifts necessary in this line of work. I have tried several times, but have been let down and also there is the cost factor.

86

'I used to be like that'

I have recently started my son on solids, and I am looking into making my own meals for him. It is much cheaper for me to buy extra fruit and vegetables than it is to buy special babyfood. I know exactly what he's eaten, and know that he's not getting any artificial flavours or colours. I've estimated it would cost me £10 a week to feed him on jars and tins, which would use all his Child Benefit up. I recently started putting a portion of veg. aside from ours, so I could freeze it for use when he's ready. To save money I use my breastmilk storage jars to put the tiny amounts in.

I also use terry nappies as they pay for themselves after a few weeks. I have some disposable nappies to use at night – as he sleeps through, I want him to wear something more absorbent. Terries are definitely cheaper, when you think I used to spend £6 a week on nappies. The only other things that I have to buy him are clothes, mainly vests. He is four months old but is wearing six–twelve-month sizes. He is quite long, so once the clothes get too short in the legs or body, we have to get some more.

When I was pregnant I didn't earn much at all, but I used to buy bits and pieces for the baby, and it soon mounts up. But once the baby's here they grow so fast, so you still have expenses. I'm lucky in that Tom's Nan knits him cardigans and blankets, so that saves money. We are not poor by any standards but like most people we don't have money for any luxuries at the end of the day.

I remember when I just had Tom and I was coming out of the

supermarket with the groceries and I saw a group of girls laughing and chatting. It suddenly dawned on me, 'I used to be like that.' You definitely grow up once your baby's here, and your priorities change. I have suffered with the 'postnatal blues', even though I have a loving partner and family. At times it is daunting, being responsible for another human being who depends on you so much, so I suppose it takes a while for your emotions to adjust.

I will probably return to work as a registered childminder simply so I can help my partner with the bills and so I have some money for myself. I think when you have a baby you forget your needs, as you're so focused on them.

87

'Good luck to the mothers of the twenty-first century'

A brief history of my own childhood will, I think, let you see why I am able to deal with the financial storms of current family life. I am 31 years old now and I grew up in the sixties and seventies. From the age of six I was the eldest of three children in a single-parent family. At this time we lived in council property and were brought up on Social Security. As a child I was always fully aware of our family's financial and social position. As a result, I never asked our mother for expensive toys or informed her of school outings or holidays.

Throughout my school days, society was also aware of my family's position. I stood in a separate dinner-money queue in order to use my benefits voucher and I was often publicly reminded about the school charity-clothes box! These memories, which I hope have made me less judgemental of people, have given me a determination not to ever place my two wonderful daughters in such a position. I hope they will be able to grow up with fewer worries and concerns in their childhood.

For many, my present circumstances will seem a step up socially, and indeed in many ways they are. I now live in a house owned (on mortgage) by myself and my husband. I started studying for a degree this year to enable me to pursue a career in teaching once my youngest daughter is established at school. My husband works long hours running his own business and we live in the affluent South! However, my own improved circumstances place my family in the position of having, on average, 47p spare each week! Despite having to ensure I do not overspend our weekly budget I am relieved because we are not in debt, but it also requires each week's money to be strictly allocated.

Our home doesn't have any form of central heating, no tumble dryer, dishwasher or microwave. I make our clothes (or buy second-hand), all our furniture is second-hand and revamped by us. I make all our soft furnishings, preserves, and we don't have sweets, biscuits and cakes. Roast chicken or pork on a Sunday lasts until Wednesday (with chicken I stock the bones for Thursday). The children and I make our birthday cards and as many presents as possible and as a family we don't have pension and basic insurance schemes (which is a cause for concern). Unfortunately for us, we earn just too much to qualify for any form of benefit payment so we have to pay all our bills. As a housewife I can't qualify for a grant because I am unable to register as unemployed. Come this summer I will have to work around my two-year-old and find part-time work to fund my education. It is seemingly impossible to register with a NHS dentist, consequently my husband and I haven't seen a dentist for eighteen months. There have been times when emergencies have arisen (i.e., prescriptions), when I have had to forgo sanitary items and use cheap tissues! My children have a more secure childhood than I did but they are having to learn to appreciate money because we are careful about managing it, and thankfully my daughters accommodate my refusal to bow to commercial pressures regarding the 'in' toy or 'designer' labels.

It seems to me that unless you have a very good or double income for your family, the nineties family will always struggle. I know I will have to go out to work to give our family financial security. Despite this I am torn between the need to work and the desire and delight I get from being at home for my children whilst they are young. I often wonder if the politicians have any idea of the real standards of living for the majority of average families. I want my children to have aspirations and a real chance of a secure life but to do this it seems that life's path has to be calculated and planned! Lifestyles aren't as primitive now, that's progress, and expectations on quality of lifestyle have changed, but from my experience a mother of the nineties still has to be adaptable, flexible and very resourceful in order to keep a sense of pride and strength within her family.

Good luck to the mothers of the twenty-first century.

Maternity into the Twenty-First Century: the Policy of the Maternity Alliance

Mother Courage is an end-of-the-century sequel to *Maternity: Letters from Working Women*, which was published in 1915 by the Women's Co-operative Guild. The Guild was founded in 1883, when working-class women had no public voice, and it quickly became one of the first women's groups to campaign for maternity benefits and services, and improved infant and child-care facilities. By the time of the First World War, there were 32,000 Guildswomen.

Maternity influenced the campaign for improved maternity services and for the National Health Service. One of *Mother Courage*'s editors, Margaret Wynn, was two years old when it was published. She first heard *Maternity* quoted by a miner's daughter when her school had its own election, imitating the General Election of 1929. In her student days during the Depression, she quoted it as moving evidence of the plight of working-class women and what the feminists of her day were fighting against. Years later, with her own two-year-old daughter on her knee, she sat in her local Women's Co-operative Guild, at meeting after meeting, discussing the Beveridge Report and the plans for a National Health Service that would make *Maternity* a history at last. And in many respects they did. But there was still much to do: for example, in 1979 perinatal and neonatal mortality were twice as high in the lowest socio-economic classes as in the highest. In 1980 Margaret Wynn helped to found the Maternity Alliance.

The Maternity Alliance was founded to improve and increase the support given to parents and their babies before conception, during pregnancy and in the first year of life. It was created by over seventy national organizations, led by the National Council for One Parent Families, Child Poverty Action Group and The Spastics Society, now renamed Scope. We believe not only in the right of women to choose where and how to give birth, but, most importantly, in the need to address the economic and social factors which directly and indirectly determine women's experience of pregnancy and the health of the baby.

Maternity care cannot be isolated from these social issues. As the letters in this book testify and the statistics in the Appendix show, poverty and other adverse social and environmental factors affect the life chances, health and wellbeing of many babies and their mothers. Policies can be applied to change these conditions. We believe that most infant deaths and ill health are avoidable. In particular, through a programme of campaigns, legal action, information, research and training, we focus on women and families with special needs, believing that services which get things right for them will result in improvements for everyone.

The Maternity Alliance has a vision of a better future for all pregnant women, new parents and their babies. It is only when specific policies are introduced in the context of an overall programme of support for pregnant women that the legacy of piecemeal change can be overcome. Current policies are often complex and inconsistent. In 1996 pregnant women are entitled to fourteen weeks maternity leave but eighteen weeks Statutory Maternity Pay; the Department of Health recommends breast-feeding for a minimum of four months, yet many women have to return to work when their babies are only a few weeks old; the Department of Social Security sets benefit levels which are not sufficient to buy the food pregnant women are recommended to eat; women spend less and less time in hospital after their babies are born but many return to inadequate or temporary housing where they have no help at all.

Right from the Start

No baby should be born poor. In the 1990s nearly one baby in every three is born into a family living on means-tested benefits. Income Support, the weekly allowance for those not in work or without enough to live on, is paid to young pregnant women at a lower rate, and most pregnant sixteen- and seventeen-year-olds receive no benefit until late in their pregnancy. Many students and refugees receive nothing at all. The £100 Social Fund Maternity Payment is all that many of the poorest mothers have to buy the things they need for a new baby; the Maternity Grant for all new mothers has been abolished entirely. The Department of Social Security cannot demonstrate that it is possible to buy an adequate diet on present benefit levels. Babies who are born too soon or too small are more likely than others to die or be in poor health in childhood or even in later life. The percentage of live-born babies weighing under 2,500 grams or 5½ lb. at birth has shown little sign of declining over the past forty years. In any given year it ranges from under 6 per cent in some affluent areas to 9 per cent or more in some inner-city areas. Low birthweight is more common in families where the father is in a manual occupation or there is no father than in those with a father in a non-manual occupation.

The sheer cost of having a baby and the interest of us all in the health and wellbeing of babies and those who care for them must be reflected in policy in all areas of life.

- All pregnant women must have an adequate income.

- No pregnant women should face maternity living in poverty.

- Benefit levels must be sufficient to purchase an adequate diet.

- There should be a premium for pregnancy added to Income Support from confirmation of pregnancy.

- All pregnant women, whatever their age, should receive Income Support at the full rate.

- The £100 Maternity Payment from the Social Fund must be increased to reflect the real cost of a baby.
- The government should give priority to developing strategies for reducing levels of low birthweight and the ill-health associated with it.

Work and Home

The majority of parents and parents-to-be are in paid employment or would like to be. However, women still pay the highest price for having children, in terms of loss of income and employment opportunities, and there is no statutory right to let fathers have time off work to care for their babies. The system of Statutory Maternity Pay and leave is intended to enable women to be absent from work in order to have a baby and to ensure that the baby flourishes. But the present provisions are extraordinarily complicated. A law lord has described them as 'of inordinate complexity exceeding the worst excesses of a taxing statute . . . which is especially regrettable bearing in mind that they regulate the everyday rights of ordinary employers and employees'. Women on the lowest incomes receive no Statutory Maternity Pay at all. And how can you maintain breast-feeding if you have to return to work when your baby is just a few weeks old?

- There should be a comprehensive, coherent system of statutory maternity, paternity and parental rights at work.
- This should include an adequate, paid paternity or nominated-carer leave to allow a partner to play a full part in the care of the new baby.
- All women should have an adequate period of paid maternity leave after the birth to ensure breast-feeding and the care of mother and baby.
- Maternity and paternity leave should be followed by paid parental leave.

- Leave for family reasons will enable parents to take time off work when a baby is ill or for clinic appointments.

- All women should be paid an adequate allowance while on maternity leave.

Welcome to the World

Every half an hour a baby is born to a family living in temporary accommodation or housing unfit for a baby to be brought home to. Compared with fifty years ago, grandparents tend to live further away. Women who give birth in hospital leave sooner after the birth and there is less help at home for families with new babies.

- All families should have decent living conditions.

- Before women are discharged from hospital to go home, support must be ensured.

- The home-help system should be strengthened, especially for mothers who are disabled or have multiple births.

- All parents should have access to the best available maternity services and should have information and choices before, during and after pregnancy.

- Education for midwives, doctors and health visitors should reflect the fact that pregnant women's take-up of health care and ability to follow advice offered is affected by their social and economic circumstances and by wider social, financial and health-care policies.

Maternity: Letters from Working Women was by women who believed that writing about their lives would help other families. 'If there is anything else you would like to know and I could tell you, I should be glad, for the benefit of my sisters,' wrote one woman. The women who contributed to *Mother Courage* wrote for the same reason, and many ended their letters with comments like 'I hope these notes might be of some help. I have tried to suggest some of my concerns with what could be made easier for parents.' They, too, hope to see conditions improve for future mothers and their families. The last letter ends: 'Good luck to the mothers of the twenty-first century.'

APPENDIX:

Figures Bearing on Maternity Poverty

ALISON MACFARLANE

There is no official definition of poverty, but parents who live on means-tested benefits and are therefore eligible for maternity payments of £100 from the Social Fund experience very severe financial difficulties. Nearly a third of the babies born in the early and mid 1990s were born to parents in this category. Figure 1 shows that this applied to just over a quarter of babies born in

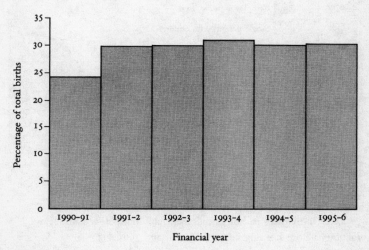

Source: Department of Social Security, Office for National Statistics, General Register Office Scotland

Figure 1 Maternity payments from the social fund as a percentage of total births in Great Britain

Britain in the financial year 1990–91, rising to 30 per cent of babies born in 1991–2. The proportion was still 30 per cent in 1995–6.

Children in Low-Income Households

The gap between the two extremes of income distribution widened during the 1980s as a result of rising unemployment and decreases in taxation on the people with the highest incomes.[1] This has led to considerable increases since 1980 in the numbers of people in households which include children and whose total income is less than half of the national average household income, as Figure 2 shows.

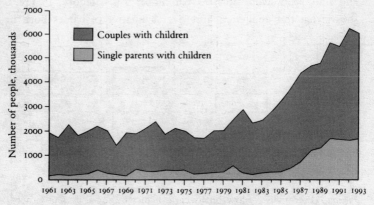

Source: Analysis of Office for National Statistics Family Expenditure Survey data by the Institute of Fiscal Studies

Figure 2 Individuals in households with children below half average income, before housing costs, Great Britain, 1961–93

Birthweight and Social Class

Babies with fathers in manual occupations are more likely to be born small than those with fathers in non-manual occupations.

This can be either because they are born too soon, or because they are growth-retarded. The World Health Organisation's official definition of low birthweight is weighing under 2500 grams, or 5½ lbs. Using this definition, 4.7 per cent of babies born alive in 1994 with fathers in professional occupations were of low birthweight, compared with 8 per cent of babies with fathers in unskilled manual occupations, as Figure 3 shows. For babies registered by their mothers alone, 9.5 per cent were of low birthweight.

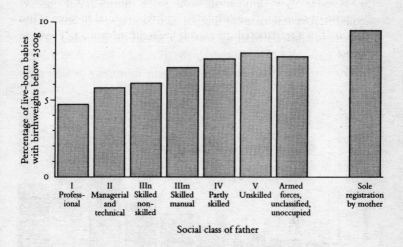

Source: Office for National Statistics, Mortality Statistics, series DH3

Figure 3 Percentage of low-birthweight babies by social class of father, England and Wales, 1994
(Births within marriage and jointly registered births outside marriage)

Infant Mortality and Social Class

Infant mortality, defined as deaths of live-born babies before the age of one year, has declined throughout the twentieth century in England and Wales. Since 1905, deaths in the first month after live birth, now known as neonatal deaths, have been counted separately from deaths occurring after a month but under a year, which are now known as postneonatal deaths.

Neonatal mortality rates have declined steadily throughout the twentieth century, from 41.8 deaths per thousand live births in England and Wales in 1905 to 4.1 in 1995.[2] Postneonatal mortality rates were very high at the beginning of this century, with marked peaks coinciding with hot summers when diarrhoeal disease was a major killer. The postneonatal mortality rate of 2.0 per thousand live births in 1995 is just over a fiftieth of the rate of 86.4 per thousand live births in 1905.[3] Improvements in public health and the socio-economic circumstances of the population as a whole have made an outstanding contribution to this decrease in mortality. These factors have also contributed to the fall in childhood mortality. Over the five-year period 1906–1910, the death rate among chil-

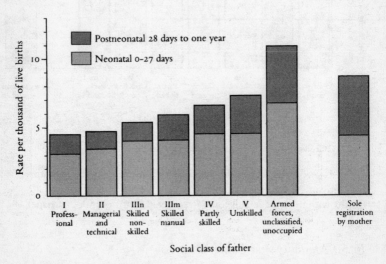

Source: OPCS Monitor DH3 95/1

Figure 4 Infant mortality by social class of father, England and Wales, 1994 (Births within marriage and jointly registered births outside marriage)

dren aged one to four years was 17.2 per thousand population, compared to 0.4 in the five-year period 1986–90.[4]

It is virtually impossible to make a link between data about income and data about social class based on parents' occupations, which are used in analyses of data from birth and death registration. In addition, births outside marriage have only been routinely tabulated by social class since 1993, making it impossible to look at trends over time. All that can be said is that the data show that inequalities persist. Figure 4 shows social class differences in infant mortality, which are particularly wide in the postneonatal period, while Figure 5 shows similar differences in stillbirth rates.[5]

Despite the recent decline, as many as 30 per cent of postneonatal deaths in 1994 were attributed to Sudden Infant Death Syndrome. Such deaths are often referred to as 'cot deaths'. Data published

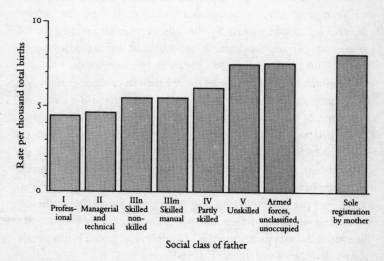

Source: OPCS Monitor DH3 95/1

Figure 5 Stillbirth rates by social class of father, England and Wales, 1994 (Births within marriage and jointly registered births outside marriage)

by the Confidential Enquiry into Stillbirths and Deaths in Infancy showed wide social differences between the families whose babies died and control babies selected from the same health visitors' lists.[6] For example, two-thirds of the parents whose babies died were receiving Income Support or other benefits, compared with 28 per cent of the families of controls. Of the babies who died, 45 per cent came from families where neither parent was employed, compared with only 15 per cent of the controls.

The Changing Family

Families are much smaller in the 1990s than they were at the beginning of this century. The 1911 census showed that married women in England and Wales born between 1861 and 1865 had had an average of 4.66 live births. A survey after the Second World War showed that women married in the years 1910–1914 had had an average of 2.90.[7] Contemporary data show that the average number of children born by the time a woman reached 45 fell from 2.26 per woman born in 1929 to 2.08 per woman born in 1949.[8] This downward trend appears to be continuing.

The letters in *Mother Courage* show a pattern of single parenthood and changing relationships in the 1990s. Apart from the two post-war periods, the extent to which births took place outside marriage was fairly static until the early 1960s, as Figure 6 shows, with 4.4 per cent of live births occurring outside marriage in 1915 and 4.7 per cent in 1955.[9] Since then, the proportion of births outside marriage has risen steeply to 7.7 per cent in 1965, 9.1 per cent in 1975, 19.2 per cent in 1985 and 33.9 per cent in 1995. Nevertheless, over three-quarters of these births were registered by both parents in 1995 and about three-quarters of couples registering births jointly stated that they lived at the same address.

The extent to which births registered by both parents took place outside marriage varies across the social spectrum, as measured by the father's social class. This is illustrated in Figure 7, which shows that in 1994 only a tenth of births to fathers with professional

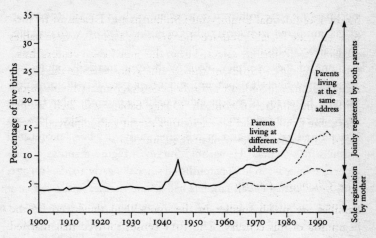

Source: Office for National Statistics, Birth statistics, Series FM 1

Figure 6 Live births outside marriage, England and Wales, 1990–1995

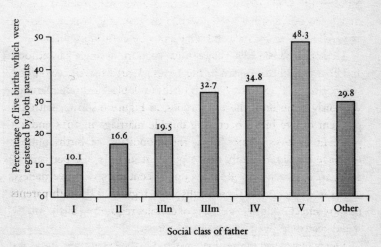

Source: OPCS Monitor, DH3 95/1

Figure 7 Percentage of live births taking place outside marriage by social class of father, England and Wales, 1994

Appendix

occupations were jointly registered by both parents outside marriage, compared with nearly a half of births to fathers with unskilled manual occupations.[10]

Some of these couples, along with some married couples, are increasingly likely to split up, and other parents will form new couples. Since the 1970s, the extent of single parenthood in families with dependent children under the age of sixteen, or aged between sixteen and eighteen and in full-time study, has been monitored through the General Household Survey.[11] Figure 8 shows a considerable increase in lone parenthood since the early 1970s. In 1971, only 7 per cent of such families had a lone mother and 1 per cent a lone father. By 1994, 21 per cent of families had a lone mother – with 8 per cent single, 1 per cent widowed, 7 per cent separated and 5 per cent divorced – while 2 per cent of families had a lone father. The proportion of mothers who were divorced or separated rose steadily over the years, but the proportion who were single increased sharply during the 1980s, from 2 per cent in 1981 to 6 per cent in 1991.

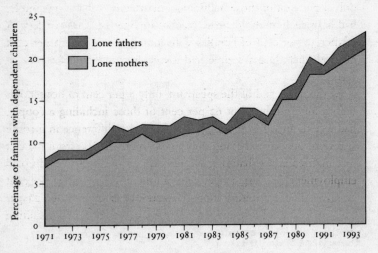

Source: Office for National Statistics, General Household Survey

Figure 8 Families with lone parents, Great Britain, 1971–94

In 1994, 20 per cent of children in Great Britain were in families with lone mothers: 6 per cent were in families with one dependent child and 14 per cent in families with two or more dependent children. The youngest child was in the 0–4 year age group in 43 per cent of households with lone mothers and 44 per cent of households with married or cohabiting couples. The families with lone fathers had a different age structure, with only 14 per cent of their youngest members being in the 0–4 year age group.[12]

There were considerable differences in the housing of lone-parent and other families. Just over a third of lone parents were owner-occupiers, compared with just over three-quarters of other families. Only 7 per cent lived in a detached house, compared with 24 per cent of other families. In contrast, 23 per cent of lone-parent families and only 7 per cent of other families lived in a flat or maisonette.[13]

On average, single-parent families are worse off than two-parent families. In 1994, 47 per cent of families with lone mothers, but only 4 per cent of those including a married or cohabiting couple, had a usual household gross weekly income of £100 or less. A further 30 per cent of families with lone mothers and 12 per cent of those including a couple had a weekly income of £100.01 to £200.[14]

At the other end of the spectrum, only 8 per cent of households with a lone mother, but 62 per cent of those including a couple, had weekly incomes above £350. This major difference in income arises not only from having only one parent, but also from the fact that married and cohabiting women are more likely to be in paid employment. In 1994, 17 per cent of lone mothers and 24 per cent of married or cohabiting mothers worked full-time, while 23 per cent of lone mothers and 42 per cent of married or cohabiting mothers worked part-time.

Country of Birth and Ethnic Origin

In 1911, the census showed that over 96 per cent of the population of England and Wales was born there.[15] A further 2 per cent was born in Scotland, Ireland or 'islands in the British seas', which were the Isle of Man and the Channel Islands. About 0.4 per cent of the population was born in the British colonies or India. Many of these were born there to expatriate colonial administrators. Just over 1 per cent of the population were from what were described as 'foreign' countries – many from Eastern Europe.

Britain today is a much more diverse society and there are more statistics to document the extent of this. In 1994, 12.4 per cent of live births in England and Wales were to women born outside the United Kingdom.[16] These included 0.8 per cent to women born in Ireland, 0.5 per cent to women born in the 'Old Commonwealth' countries of Australia, Canada and New Zealand, and 7.1 per cent to women born in what is described as the 'New Commonwealth'. This, in turn, included 1.1 per cent of live births to women born in India, 1.9 per cent to women born in Pakistan, 0.9 per cent to women born in Bangladesh, 1.6 per cent to women born in Africa, 0.5 per cent to women born in the Caribbean Commonwealth and 0.5 per cent to women born in the Far East. These figures understate the extent of births to women descended from people born in these countries, as they only identify births to women who were themselves born in these countries. In an attempt to obtain an estimate of this, the 1991 census included a question on self-reported ethnic origin.[17]

Care during Childbirth and Afterwards

Before the First World War, very few women (probably just over 1 per cent) gave birth in charitable lying-in hospitals or in workhouse infirmaries. Everyone else gave birth at home. The percentage of live births in England and Wales taking place in institutions of some sort rose from 15 per cent in 1927 to 24 per cent in 1932 and 34.8 per cent in 1937.[18] By 1946, over half of all births took place in institutions.[19] By 1970, only 12 per cent of deliveries took place at home. This fell to an all-time low of 0.9 per cent in 1987 and most births now take place in hospitals with consultant obstetric units. Since then there has been a steady but slight increase in the proportion of births at home, reaching 1.9 per cent of all deliveries in 1995.

Although the statistics for England are unreliable, they suggest that in the financial year 1994–5 15 per cent of deliveries were by caesarean section and a further 11 per cent were instrumental deliveries by forceps or vacuum extraction.[20] More reliable data for Scotland for the same financial year show that 15.8 per cent of single births were by caesarean section, 8.1 per cent by forceps and 3.3 per cent by vacuum extraction.[21]

An important item on the Women's Co-operative Guild's agenda was help in the home for women after childbirth, and legislation passed in 1915 gave local authorities power to provide this. Over thirty years later, a survey of a week's births in 1946 found that only 1.6 of women who delivered had a 'municipal' home-help, although 70 per cent said they would like such help for their next birth.[22] There are few places today where home-helps are provided for women with new babies. In the late 1980s, 39 per cent of mothers of triplets questioned in a survey reported that they had no local-authority home-help.[23]

Women's Health after Childbirth

Pregnancy is no longer life threatening for most women. In 1915, official figures recorded 5.27 deaths directly or indirectly associated with childbearing for every thousand live births in England and Wales.[24] In 1995 the figure was 0.072 per thousand total births,[25] just over 1.3 per cent of the rate for 1915.

Although women today are unlikely to experience as many severe health problems as women in 1915, it is difficult to assess their extent. In particular, there are few statistics about the health of women after they give birth, although surveys show that health problems which are not life threatening are still widespread.[26] The problems include pain, breast and bleeding problems, bowel irregularities, tiredness and depression. A survey which followed up 11,701 women who delivered in a Birmingham hospital showed that about four-fifths of them experienced pain in the shoulders, limbs or back, migraine, incontinence or piles, with symptoms lasting over three months. Many of them also experienced depression and fatigue.[27]

Interpreting the Figures

When collecting letters from its members in 1914, the Women's Co-operative Guild asked women how many children, miscarriages and stillbirths they had had and how many of their children had died during childhood. This time round, the editors did not ask such questions. Instead, official statistics have been used to provide background information. These statistics make it clear that the writers of the letters in this book, while not a random sample, are not atypical of many mothers of young children in Britain today.

Alison Macfarlane is Medical Statistician at the National Perinatal Epidemiology Unit, Radcliffe Infirmary, Oxford.

Alison Macfarlane's research is funded by the Department of Health.

NOTES

1. A. Goodman, S. Webb, 'For Richer, for Poorer. The Changing Distribution of Income in the United Kingdom, 1961–91', IFS Commentary no. 42 (London: Institute for Fiscal Studies, 1994).

2. A. J. Macfarlane, M. Mugford, *Birth Counts: Statistics of Pregnancy and Childbirth* (London: HMSO, 1984); Office for National Statistics, 'Mortality Statistics: Cause' series DH2, published annually; Office

for National Statistics, 'Mortality Statistics: Perinatal and Infant: Social and Biological Factors', series DH3, published annually.

3. Office for National Statistics, 'Mortality Statistics: Cause': Office for National Statistics, 'Mortality Statistics: Perinatal and Infant: Social and Biological Factors'.

4. Office for National Statistics, 'Mortality Statistics: Cause'.

5. Office for National Statistics, 'Mortality Statistics: Perinatal and Infant: Social and Biological Factors'.

6. Confidential Enquiry into Stillbirths and Deaths in Infancy, third annual report, 1 January–31 December 1994 (London: Department of Health, 1996).

7. A. J. Macfarlane, M. Mugford, 'Birth Counts: Statistics of Pregnancy and Childbirth'; Royal Commission on Population, Report, cmnd 7695 (London: HMSO, 1949).

8. Office for National Statistics, 'Birth Statistics', series FM1, published annually.

9. Ibid.

10. Office for National Statistics, 'Mortality Statistics: Perinatal and Infant: Social and Biological Factors'.

11. Office of Population Censuses and Surveys, 'Living in Britain. Results from the 1994 General Household Survey' (London: HMSO, 1996).

12. Ibid.

13. Ibid.

14. Ibid.

15. General Register Office, Census of England and Wales, 1911, Vol. IX, Birthplaces, cd 7017 (London: HMSO, 1913).

16. Office for National Statistics, 'Birth Statistics'.

17. Office of Population Censuses and Surveys, 1991 Census, ethnic group and country of birth (London: HMSO, 1993).

18. R. Campbell, A. J. Macfarlane, *Where to Be Born? The Debate and the Evidence*, second edition (Oxford: National Perinatal Epidemiology Unit, 1994).

19. Joint Committee of the Royal College of Obstetricians and the Population Investigation Committee, *Maternity in Great Britain* (London: Oxford University Press, 1948).

20. Department of Health, Maternity Hospital Episode Statistics.

21. Information and Statistics Division, Scottish Health Statistics 1995 (Edinburgh: ISD, 1995).

22. Joint Committee of the Royal College of Obstetricians and the Population Investigation Committee, *Maternity in Great Britain*

23. B. Botting, A. J. Macfarlane, F. Price (eds.), *Three, Four and More. A Study of Triplet and Higher Order Births* (London: HMSO, 1990).

24. A. J. Macfarlane, M. Mugford, *Birth Counts: Statistics of Pregnancy and Childbirth*.

25. Office for National Statistics, 'Mortality and Statistics: Cause'; Office for National Statistics, 'Mortality Statistics: Perinatal and Infant: Social and Biological Factors'.

26. C. M. A. Glazener, C. MacArthur, J. Garcia, 'Postnatal Care: Time for a Change', *Contemporary Reviews in Obstetrics and Gynaecology*, 1993, 5, 130–36.

27. C. MacArthur, M. Lewis, E. G. Knox, *Health after Childbirth* (London: HMSO, 1991).